Ring Around Racing

Thom Ring

Ring, Thom
Ring Around Racing

SUMMARY: collection of columns previously published in newspapers and magazines.

set in Times New Roman

Cover photo by Leif Tillotson of Joey Polewarczyk, Jr., in *American/Canadian Tour* action at Vermont's Thunder Road Speedbowl.

YankeePress
Burrillville, RI

CONTENTS

ALMOST FAST

Early in 2008, midget car-owner Don Douville gave me a chance to race one of his midget racecars at Whip City Speedway, a quarter-mile bullring formerly located in Westfield, Mass.

It was an incredible offer, but Don wanted to publicize the division he'd created there for low-buck midgets powered by a race-inspired motor developed by Oldsmobile. The idea was that I'd write about it for Shorttrack, *the magazine I once published, which I did. Things got even crazier when he offered to give me enough ratty old pieces to build a whole car, so I could feature the cars over the course of a season. I jumped at the chance.*

Talk about bad karma. Since the deal was struck, Oldsmobile has been shut down by General Motors, Shorttrack *was shut down by me, and Whip City was shut down by the town of Westfield, which chose not to renew the lease to the track, built on town property. The following piece is from my stillborn story,* ALMOST FAST.

My brother Ward and I finally put a car together, Don Douville let us keep what we'd built, and a pack of guys are racing these things up at Bear Ridge Speedway in Vermont as well as elsewhere on dirt and pavement.)

W e're all would-be racers.

And not just would-be racers. All sports fans are wanna-bees. They might not be playing the game, but you'd be hard-pressed to convince them they're not in it. They refer to their favorite team in the first-person, as in, "We need a new quarterback." They wear the jersey or the cap. They plot trades their team will never make. They join fantasy leagues so they can make the trades themselves.

Racefans choose their heroes and race along with them, their jackets matching their favorite driver's suit right down to the sponsor-patches. They shake their fists when their driver is cut off – or extend the same finger the driver does. They paint their radio-control or slot car to match the car their hero drives. Some racefans even have resorted to fantasy-racing leagues, an idea that makes no sense at all when adapted to this mano-a-mano sport. But it at least allows them to make a few moves, root for their own selves, and experience some sort of victory related to racing.

None of this ever worked for me. I've never rooted for any driver. While many have earned my admiration – thrilled me – they always were just guys out there doing their thing while I was a guy in the stands watching them do it. If they were cut off that was their problem, not mine. Their finger as well. My slot car wasn't painted to look like Petty's racecar, it was painted to look like my racecar. Well - it was my racecar.

As for fantasy leagues – well – wrong fantasy. Yes, I was a would-be racer, but racing is experienced not by keyboard but by the seat of the pants. I never wanted to be a racer. I wanted to race, to get out there, to go fast.

So what was stopping me? Well, I was thwarted by a common villain. Money was keeping me off the track, specifically the fact that others had it and I didn't. At least that's what I believed.

I did manage to dabble a few times. At the age of 17 I rebuilt an obsolete old Yamaha dirtbike and attempted a few motocross races, learning fast that I was not. I also learned that I lacked the dedication necessary to thrive in this sport of obscenely intense physical demands. A few years later my buddy Dave Belanger and I rebuilt his obsolete old Yamaha woods bike to share as a flat-tracker. It was profoundly out of place for the application. Indeed, the biggest thrill we got came from the impressed surprise of the tech inspectors when they realized there was no way they could rule we were illegal. Still, the fairy-tale was over by the time we hit the track, and soon Dave proved to be even less dedicated than I was. He converted his bike back to woods specs and I was out of a ride.

A decade or so later I scrounged together enough cash to get my hands on an obsolete old kart chassis and engine. Thus began my primary racing adventure competing on the tiny oval of Pomfret, Conn., Speedway after Dave and I rebuilt – or maybe I should say restored – the machine. We had so much fun with the old sled my first season that Dave went out and bought a brand-new machine. In his first race, the last of the year at Pomfret, he finished ahead of me. I took a ride in his kart, realized immediately how a kart was supposed to work, and finagled a franchise from a kart-builder so I could purchase an unassembled kart from them at cost. Hey, I almost sold one kart for them. Other than mine, I mean.

My most glorious racing experience came early the next season when, after a few races tangled up with the competition, I got the holeshot in a feature and never looked back on the way to the checkered flag. The thrill was compounded when I learned after my victory-lap that Dave had done a banzai at the finish line, putting two wheels in the infield to steal second. We laughed and hugged each other as if we'd won Le Mans. There might have been no champagne or cheering-throngs to spray it on, but who cared? We were racers.

Soon enough, though, Dave lost his job – and interest. I gained a girlfriend – and a new excuse. And kart racing, it's only fair to note, began to turn into another venue for racers who could buy what they couldn't learn. When I looked to get back into karting years later, the classes of reliable old Yamaha two-strokes we had raced in had virtually disappeared in favor of flathead lawnmower engines tricked out to turn F-1 revs, with maintenance-demands that rivaled Formula-1 as well. Furthermore, the days of karts hanging out of pickup beds had given way to enclosed trailers filled with a chassis for every day of the week, plus two on Sundays. Karting had become just another form of racing, with a money-be-damned attitude that betrayed its humble roots.

Not that I didn't have at least one forgettable foray back into karting. I'd heard about a series taking place on the inner oval at Stafford Motor

Speedway, so I refitted my kart to meet what I understood of the rules. With Dave and his van no longer available I bought one of those put-it-together-yourself utility trailers and bolted a hitch to my Ford Escort. Really. Then I loaded up the Escort with my tools, every gear and spare I had, and my eleven-year old daughter Marcy and headed toward Stafford via the hills and dales of eastern Connecticut.

Do I have to tell you how it went at Stafford? I guess I do. First of all we got there an hour and a half later than I'd planned, thanks to the hills and dales of eastern Connecticut and the rapidly fading compression of my Escort's engine. We were a sight, pulling late into the pits and parking among the enclosed trailers and canopies. Trying to find the tech guy so I could get the little green sticker that would enable me to get on the track caused me to miss my class's only practice session, so I lined up for the heat race without ever having turned a lap. This, of course, is a bad idea, even if you're uber-racer Ted Christopher and you've run at Stafford 247 times. I, on the other hand, was about to get introduced to Stafford for the first time.

Now, it's fair to say that Stafford's small oval doesn't get quite the attention that its half-mile does, and this was before the big track was repaved. But I must say, the last time I had experienced as much air-time racing as I did that day at Stafford I was on my motocross bike. The transition from the big track's front straight into turn-one was particularly teeth-crunching. Kart-crunching, too, karts being, after all, suspension-less. Entering turn-one you wound up with all four wheels literally airborne before crashing back to asphalt. Fortunately my gearing was so far off I was a quarter-lap behind the rest of the field when one landing caused me not only to throw my drive-chain but the entire two-piece rear sprocket as well.

At first I was angry I'd evidently done such a sloppy job checking fasteners that I hadn't tightened the sprocket-nuts adequately. Then I discovered the nuts hadn't backed off. The bolts had sheared off. Now I had to scramble around to find the guy with the parts truck, who of course turned out to be the guy I'd had to find to tech my kart. Any time I might have used making adjustments was therefore spent getting a sprocket back on the kart. And if you're figuring "Hey, you needed to make a gear-change, anyway," be aware I didn't have a sprocket small enough to put me anywhere near where the gearing needed to be. Neither did the parts guy, who was stocked up to serve his four-stroke clientele.

I did get back out in time for the feature. That was my private victory, which was the only one in reach by the end of what had been a really swell day. I'd spent it chasing my tail, and it was my own fault. On the other hand, if I'd wanted to practice air-time I would have done it on a dirtbike, or gone rallying. But face it. Stafford isn't set up for karts. Never mind the jump in turn-one, I wasn't even prepared for the pit entrance. No one tells you to be ready to park your kart on the side of a hill, which was what the hump over Stafford's outside-banking felt like. As for Marcy, she still hasn't forgiven me for making her lug the starter and battery around the Stafford pits. Cheez! We stopped for ice cream on the way home. What more did she want?

Yet not only did the would-be racer in me endure, I found a new way to entertain him. I'd been covering football games for my local newspaper when it announced it would begin publishing a Sunday edition. I pitched the idea of a column covering racing, and the sports editor bit. Soon I had credentials to every track in the region, including the brand-new superspeedway opening up in Loudon, NH. This was a fringe-benefit I'd anticipated when I'd pitched my column. But there was another one I hadn't imagined.

After a couple of years covering racing for the paper, I received an invitation to drive in a special "Press & Promoters'" race hosted by New Hampshire's Granite State Mini-Sprint Club on the then-dirt of Sugar Hill Speedway. The mini-sprints they raced were two-thirds the size of true midgets and powered by 500cc single-cylinder bike engines. I finagled a ride for my photographer-brother John, and we headed up to Sugar Hill.

The car I drew was campaigned by the Boisvert family and piloted by Boisvert-by-marriage Jim Dominic. The sanitary little monster was one of a horde of them built and raced by the Boisverts and offered up to racing-rubes such as me for the evening. I still can recall driving the peaky Dominic-car through the pits and realizing that this club was putting tens of thousands of dollars worth of their machinery into the hands of strangers who might or might not possess the brains to respect the opportunity they'd been given.

That was one of the two major recollections I keep from that night. The other is of having such a blast sliding the little car through Sugar Hill's corners that I was neglecting to bury the throttle for the straights. They simply were serving to connect the fun, like the climbing sections of a roller coaster. I don't recall how I finished, which leads to the obvious conclusion that it was pretty forgettable, if you haven't figured that out already.

Still, we'd had so much fun we vowed to be there the next season for the Second-Annual. Unfortunately the Second-Annual was not as much fun as the first. I drew a different car, one not nearly as well-prepared as the Boisvert loaners. The car's 250cc two-stroke engine proceeded to misfire all evening before finally dying in the feature. And I was the lucky one. John wound up in the turn-two fence, shearing off a wheel and related suspension. The car's owner was surprisingly understanding, but there never was a Third-Annual. I blame John.

Yet as much fun as I'd had driving other people's cars at Sugar Hill, the experience paled in comparison to the one I had a few years later after meeting the Boisverts at Thompson Speedway's season-ending World Series of Racing. For some bizarre reason family patriarch Armand and his son Doug had decided that season to go overboard racing via a different method than preparing and racing more cars than pass through the Ted Williams Tunnel at Thanksgiving on their way to Logan Airport. The Boisverts evidently had decided they could be just as insane running one car, but only if they jumped from the reasonable mini-sprint class all the way over every level of racing-insanity right up to the International Supermodified Association, where one car produced as much power as the 1,250 they'd campaigned at Sugar Hill.

But the Boisverts had not bitten off more than they could chew. Doug managed to drive to rookie-of-the-year honors, for one thing. And when they later put veteran Joey Payne in the car, he amply demonstrated the quality of the family's work with a number of competitive efforts and at least one victory, if memory serves.

Anyway, Armand proceeded to relate how much fun he and Doug were having and then shocked me with his next statement.

"We gotta get you into the super," he said.

For whatever reason (fear? common sense?) I didn't follow up with

14

Armand after that. But the next summer I ran into Armand again at New Hampshire Speedway. I was in my customary perch on the Armco inside the pit-row exit getting ready to watch Indy cars go at it when he hailed me from below. We exchanged the usual pleasantries while NHIS announcer Al Robinson did his pre-race spiel. Then Armand made his offer again, this time with details spelled out. I long ago had assessed the sorry state of Armand's sanity, but this was going overboard to prove the point.

I made a number of phone calls to Armand over the next few weeks, each conversation prefaced with my question, "You sure you want to do this?" He always was, but as the big day approached, Armand had a question for me.

"I have a friend who was wondering if you could do him a favor," he said.

At this point I was not about to decline to do Armand or anyone he knew any favor he requested. I agreed without even knowing what the favor was.

"My friend runs a midget," Armand explained. "He wants to know if you'd be willing to take that out, too."

You want to know how crazy this day turned out? Well, Steve Robinson, who raced the mini-sprint brother John had driven his first time at Sugar Hill, brought a car when we met up with Armand and Doug Boisvert at Canaan Speedway on a perfect autumn-in-New-Hampshire day. I was so busy driving the super and the midget I never got a chance to drive his pavement-mini.

The midget belonged to Walt Scadden. The day thus began a new friendship with one of the most interesting guys I've ever met in racing, and that's saying something. It also began my relationship with Oldsmobile's Quad-4 engine, one of which powered the midget Scadden built to tilt at the windmill that was midget racing at that time in New England. But I'm getting ahead of myself, and the memories of the day simply are too great to not revisit.

I arrived to find the three racecars parked in the pits, in wait as if they were presidential limos. After greeting the Boisverts, their friend and crew-member Armand Truchon, and Steve, and being introduced to Walt and his driver, Mike Ober, I headed into the trailer to get ready. There I found laid out before me a selection of driving suits in various sizes and styles. Armand came aboard and pointed out the cooler full of sandwiches, soda and bottled water. I met Armand's wife, Diane, who was there to time the day's runs. As I related in the article I later wrote for *Trackside Magazine*, I half-expected a bevy of Hooters Girls in heels to feed me grapes and help me don my racing duds.

A supermodified is less friendly than a Hooters Girl. I got the startup-procedure down pretty easily; the push-start with the rearend engaged, the eyes on the oil-pressure gauge until the pressure built up sufficiently, the flick of the ignition switch and tug of the fuel handle. But after that it got complicated.

I don't know if "throttle-response" is an accurate term to apply to what happens when you step on the gas in a super. Somehow the term suggests that a super interprets your input and reacts appropriately. But the throttle on the Boisvert super had no options between "idle" and "Saturn rocket screaming toward the moon." This proved a problem, because even though I could stand on it easily enough coming out of a corner (No, really. I could...) I inevitably got off the gas too early going into the next one. Then I'd try to get on it lightly, figuring I would feather it a bit through the turn, and I'd find myself heading toward the moon again.

The appearance to the highly amused bystanders might have been one of somebody learning how to drive a standard.

But on those straightaways...oh, my! It was interesting to learn later that I'd turned much faster lap times in the super than the midget, because I would have sworn I'd gone much faster in the smaller car. Indeed, the midget simply was a much easier car to drive.

A midget. Yes, what a neat deal it was that day to actually drive what perhaps was my favorite type of racecar. Midgets combine two features near and dear to my would-be racer's heart. First of all, they are thoroughbred racecars. There is not a part on a midget that pretends to do anything other than its pure racing function; no fenders, no doors, no stick-on headlights or grilles. This is a feature it shares with karts, by the way. I've never understood the attraction of making the coolest cars in the world, racecars, look like a seriously less-cool Ford Fusion. (And racing pickups? Suffice to say I will not mention them here again).

16

The midget's other great feature it also shares with karts. A midget is small. It's odd that small would be a good point about anything in America. We supposedly prefer everything bigger and bigger and bigger, including debt, apparently. I, on the other hand, can't see dragging around a pound or an inch that doesn't provide a direct functional benefit to anyone but the oil companies. Besides, it's kind of neat to be able to look over and see the guy you're racing. I'm not entirely convinced there still are real live drivers at the wheel of NASCAR stockers. Those tanks could be radio-controlled, and who would be the wiser? Maybe when they show the driver he's actually in a studio somewhere, like those oddballs who say we never went to the moon claim about astronauts.

Seriously, you can't convince me it doesn't take more skill and daring to wrap a midget around you and go racing than it does to climb through a ton-and-a-half of tubing, sheet-metal, padding, belts and nets to race a stock car, even if you are racing at double the century mark. I mean, while a stock car settles in like an asphalt-paver, midgets slip and slide all over the place even if they're racing on pavement.

Not that I did any slipping and sliding in Walt Scadden's car. But I at least felt as if I was getting the car up to speed – close to it, anyway. For one thing, true to racecar-form, as I went faster in it the Scadden midget got smoother, more predictable, more comfortable, and easier to drive. I also found some semblance of rhythm, staying on the gas, touching the brakes before I entered the corner and then feeding progressive amounts of fuel to drive on out.

Imagine my surprise, then, when I discovered I was averaging over 82 mph by the end of the day in the super while not getting close to 80 in the midget. This was by no means any fault of the midget. It was, after all, a car built for racing in Northeastern Midget Association competition, where a dollar unspent is a dollar wasted.

Yet Walt had built his car with a different approach, to say the least, more like "Any dollar spent is a dollar wasted." For one thing, when I say built, I mean built. Scadden welded up his own chassis to run against cars coming by and large from a tiny group of car-builders you could count on the fingers of one hand. While the list of builders has changed in the years since Scadden was actively competing in NEMA, the number of builders never seems to increase. It's the old adage "Nothing succeeds like success," applied to choosing equipment, where following the leader continues off the track after everyone but the winners get frustrated on it.

Walt, however, is one of those guys who will do anything to avoid following the leader in the shop, even if it only makes it harder to lead on the track. To him, as I soon learned, the challenge comes from figuring out your own way to success. To guys like him, it never comes from money. They don't have any, for one thing. Besides, it's Manhattan divas who get thrills using a charge card, not racers. Walt would turn down a top-of-the-line chassis or motor. It would defeat the whole purpose of racing. He'd be bored.

Boredom is poison to Walt Scadden. He lives about three adventures at a time and has no plans to slow down. He's accomplished so much in his life that after knowing him over a decade I'm still learning about things he's done. He's an ex-Marine, a retired firefighter, and a blacksmith of world-renown. He's built or worked on racecars in every form of the sport, from road racing to speed-runs on the salt at Bonneville. He made crash-and-burn movies for the driver-training industry. He built a wind-tunnel in a box-trailer. The list grows almost daily. He's writing books. He's at work on a car powered by compressed air. He conducts seminars on cutting louvers in sheet-metal and chopping tops on hot rods.

All of these endeavors combine Walt's interest and curiosity with some opportunity that came his way. The Quad-4 motor was another one of them, first run in the midget and then later in his beautiful belly-tank salt-flats car. Learn more about this intriguing little motor, created by General Motors's snuffed-out Oldsmobile division, and you begin to see that its challenges were right up Walt's alley.

The Quad-4 was first developed at Oldsmobile by engineers in its motorsports department, and they didn't ignore what they knew from racing. Combining a four-cylinder iron block with an aluminum cylinder-head and cam towers, the powerplant essentially blended the best features of the legendary Offenhauser and four-cylinder Cosworth racing engines. As such, it was highly developed for racing applications right out of the Olds, Chevy and Pontiac intermediates fitted with it.

Ed Wilson was among the first to see the potential of the motor back in the late 1980s. The Oklahoman was trying to find a way he could afford to move up to a midget after running karts and mini-sprints, which certainly sounds familiar. Yet Wilson didn't allow himself to be defeated by the common villain of limited funds . He was smart enough to vanquish it. He recognized the potential of the Quad-4 from the start, later being quoted with the understatement "it seemed to be overbuilt."

By then the motor already was being utilized in one of the Sports Car Club of America's "Sports Racer" classes, where it recently had replaced the aforementioned Cosworth four. But sports car racers weren't as concerned about wasting money as Wilson (I mean, those guys race for trophies in cars as expensive as modifieds). They wanted to be able to spend their considerable money on more horsepower, but SCCA officials had specified the motors be sealed. It was a match not made in heaven. The folks at Olds were open to a better one.

Enter Wilson. He had a racing buddy who worked at a GM plant and knew how to steer the idea to Olds Motor Sports. The rest, as they say, is history. Wilson first ran a Quad-4-powered midget at the 1992 Chili Bowl, that midget orgy that touches down each January in Tulsa, Oklahoma. It was not much later that Walt Scadden became intrigued by the power-potential for his own midget effort. Midget racing in New England had long been on a course of escalating expense driven from the bottoms of a precious few deep pockets. And, as with any racing club in serious need of some economical alternative-sources of power, resistance to just such an idea was equally serious. His Quad-4 midget never got a break from the powers of Northeastern midget racing. Scadden worked hard to earn a few top-ten finishes before he grew tired of running uphill all the way around the track. Besides, new challenges had caught his attention.

In the meantime, however, Don Douville was hanging in there racing his own under-funded midget, primarily with veteran racer John Ferrell in control. Don was a midget mainstay, committed to helping run NEMA for many years even while racing in the club grew increasingly beyond his means. He'd watched as his friend Walt struggled to chase the leaders with his perpetually-under-development Quad-4 motor. He'd noticed that while the motor struggled to keep up with the leaders, particularly on larger tracks, it sure seemed eager to keep on trying. He'd seen the guts of the motor, was aware of its racing pedigree. And he knew where the bones of these motors were buried. Quad-4 motors were everywhere, potentially in any small GM car that had letters like "S" or "GT" after its model-name. And he knew they could be had for cheap money.

For that matter, so could midgets. Midgets were everywhere. They'd been built for years, after all. So many Ed Wilsons and Don Douvilles had succumbed to the lure of midget racing, only to find that racing a midget was sort of like dating a movie star, a fine fantasy but a crazy and expensive practice in real life. And unlike movie stars, who remarried, many of the midgets had been parked and forgotten.

Don was sure that enough midgets and Quad-4 mills could be brought together to create a new division of midgets for guys like him who could not or would not chase the escalating costs of midget racing. What he needed was a track on which to race them. Enter Whip City Speedway.

Anyone into racing should enter Whip City Speedway. For one thing, Whip City is the only dirt track in southern New England and one of the few in New England at all. Every fan needs to see dirt-track racing at least once. They may decide they like it more than pavement racing. I do. You see, just one car on a dirt track can provide as much excitement as a field of cars on pavement, because being hooked up on dirt really just means you're not entirely out of control.

Dirt-track racing generally is shorttrack racing, but if you get out of New England you'll see dirt ovals as large as a mile. Racing on a dirt mile is like superspeedway racing in snow. Whip City is not a superspeedway, but its quarter-mile of imported clay forces a driver to be very open-minded about the concept of traction.

I liked racing on dirt even before I drove a racecar at Sugar Hill. You can appreciate its appeal if you've ever gone sliding around on the ice and snow in a parking lot somewhere. Don't tell me you haven't. In fact, if you haven't you'd best do it the next time it snows. Then you'll realize that just because your car is sliding doesn't mean you can't control it. That could help you driving in the snow someday. I only wish more drivers knew how to do it.

You might also discover that sliding around in your car can be an absolute blast. You find yourself working hard to keep up with where your car is deciding to go. It's the old "steer in the direction of the skid," thing. What you're trying to do is keep the back of the car from passing the front of the car. On a dirt oval that's where "steer right to go left" comes in.

My first experience steering right to go left at Whip City came in the waning days of *Trackside*. I was there doing research for a story about racing there – which of course required that I race there. *Trackside's* editors had arranged for me to drive a mini-sprint driven by Carl Sherman. This class of mini was a step up from the singles at Sugar Hill. Not only was the car itself bigger, but it was motivated by a 600cc four-cylinder Suzuki street-bike motor.

An aside is warranted here. Predictably I questioned – well, if not the sanity then at least the common sense of Sherman. He was going to let me take his car out for practice as well as the heat race during an actual Saturday night points-event at The Whip. Then he'd start the feature from whatever spot on the grid I earned for him. By now my questioning of sanity was a consistent observation I was making about anyone who'd let me drive his car. Yet another could be made. These guys were all into racing for the experience of it above all. They considered watching me play havoc with their pride and joy simply as part of the fun. That says something about the purity of their racing experience, not to mention the fact that they generally were having way more fun than much of their competition.

My story about the evening was intended to focus on the experience of a night of competition; using practice to prepare for the first race, being ready to go when your division was called to the grid, getting up to speed in an instant once the green flag was unfurled, running to your capability for the entire race, and then doing it all again. But the experience of simply driving on dirt could not be ignored.

I've commented before that story and since about the difference between driving on pavement and on dirt. Racing on pavement is all about smooth precision. You're trying to run each and every lap to a carefully calculated level of perfection. You work to determine exactly when you can get on the gas, and you work to be able to grab all of your car's power as soon as you're grabbing any of it. Then you try to find the absolute last inch before you have to get on the brakes and can do it smoothly enough to not upset the delicate balance of four-wheel traction that ensures maximum speed. As soon as you brake you then want to put down as much throttle as your car will tolerate without losing traction, and the instant you cross the imaginary line where you know the car will hook up at full-throttle, you boot it.

That description actually applies to racing on dirt as well, but here's the difference. Good pavement racers can identify those points precisely on the track. Indeed, they will note physical points of reference; marks on the outside wall, divots in the infield, even spots on the asphalt. You might find it hard to believe they can do that, but it's easier than you think. Usually, once you get up to speed in a racecar you experience the sensation of everything slowing down around you. At first the pavement might be whizzing by in a blur, but soon you notice that the things rushing by start to come into focus. Now you can see the marks on the wall or fence.

There's a story famous within European road-racing circles of Englishman Sir Stirling Moss roaming the pits after a practice-session looking for a particularly fine-looking woman in a particular dress. When he found her she was amazed. Where she'd been standing, cars had been flying by at well in excess of 100 mph. Let's hope she was similarly impressed. Moss always was a lady's man.

I'd bet famed sprint car driver Steve Kinser experiences similarly acute vision traveling in excess of 100 mph on one of those dirt miles. Beyond that, though, his and any dirt-racing effort does not duplicate the smooth precision of the pavement racer. For one thing, the points move. It's dirt, after all. But there's more to it than that. You've likely watched enough Cup racing to hear about how the track is changing over the course of the 500 miles, four hours, 709 commercials and 151 yellow flags of the race. In a 50-lap shorttrack race, that's not really happening. Your braking point on the first lap is your braking point on the 41st.

On the dirt things can change – every lap. And you won't know it. You'll have your car exactly where you had it a lap ago, but where it hooked up sweet then it decides to swap ends now. So while it tracked through the corner as if it was on rails a lap ago you're fighting to keep it inside the fence this time. It's the same accelerating. Maybe the rear wheels sank their teeth into the track the last time out. Now they're sitting there throwing dirt on the turn-four spectators or again looking to swap ends.

Furthermore, forget lines. Yeah, on pavement he's on the inside line so you take the outside and the two of you motor through the corner like a couple of slot cars. But on dirt his inside line ends up an outside line by the time he's into the corner and you end up in the fence – or diving under him because you came into the corner outside him.

So what does this all mean? Well, you try to be smooth and you try to be precise but what you're really trying to do is hang on, making it all up as you race along, every second acting and reacting to what's going on around you and underneath you. My favorite comparison is to music, pavement racing being classical music, all written out and played exactly the same by musicians reading every note and playing it as written, and dirt racing being jazz improvised note by note by a group of musicians who are making it all up as they go along. Now extend the metaphor. Dirt-racing simply is way cooler than classical music.

Driving Sherman's mini again confirmed it. I again was having a blast. Mini-sprints are amazing machines. You'd be surprised how much power one of these rice-burner motors makes, and the cars themselves don't weigh all that much more than the bikes that originally carried the motors.

I didn't do abominably, either. Most importantly I remembered my purpose there was to race. I booted it, for one thing, each time I came out of a corner. Admittedly, though, I still was dabbling, although not to the extent Carl might have expected.

"I'm impressed," he admitted after practice. "You did way better than I thought you would."

I got other feedback as well. Steve Robinson had moved on from his single-cylinder mini and was one of Carl's competitors. He'd been on the track with Carl's division during practice.

"I followed you for a while," he offered. "You had a pretty good line. You were going good."

Hey, I went all right in my race as well. I started on the inside of the third row, the fifth of six cars for some reason. A conscious decision to not floor it until the car in front of me took off meant I was well behind the pace even into the first corner. But the gap with the rest of the field didn't get notably worse for the duration of the race, and the guy in sixth was never seen again. That put me comfortably in the cradle between racers, and I never got to mix it up with other cars. Not that my race was uneventful. I recalled Carl's advice about taking the car up to the front-stretch fence – almost – and decided I should try to turn up the wick a bit as I raced under the white flag. I did. I also wound up bouncing my outside tires off the Armco, and after verbally slapping myself across the face I carefully brought the car around to the checkered flag.

Carl had a tough time in the feature and ultimately got together with another car before taking a DNF. I had nothing to do with it, I swear.

All in all the experience was a good one for me. It reinforced my high opinion of mini-sprints, for one thing. These cars packed a lot of racecar into a very small and relatively inexpensive package. My ride also served as a highly positive introduction to Whip City. The place was created primarily through the efforts of Frank Ferreira and Dave Pighetti. They didn't do it to make a ton of money. That's a bad reason to build any racetrack. What they wanted to create was a place for folks to race without going bankrupt or spending half their waking hours chasing "corporate partners." Here was a place that provided a serious playground for grownups who simply were looking to have some racing fun. No one here was out to conquer the world. Just about every class at Whip City was geared to the weekend warrior. Nor did Whip City pretend to be the minor leagues to the bigtime racing on TV. A fan could have a very enjoyable time at The Whip after entering through the front gate, but the place was built for racers, not racefans. And this wasn't like those indoor kart places that rent the experience for stratospheric prices and then present themselves as gentlemen's country clubs.

I'd had my exposure to that experience, driving in a six-hour endurance race for an ALS charity at F1 Boston, an indoor facility on the outskirts of the city. I was well aware of the upscale venue, but it took a charity before I could bring myself to spend their sort of money for a few laps in a kart when I still owned two of them and could have hours of free fun winding around procured pylons in a parking lot with a buddy or brother. Still, F1 Boston certainly was first-class all the way. The circuit was tight and twisty and the karts reliable and responsive. The fast guys there, though, were a little hard to take. Some of them took themselves way too seriously, with their quilted karting suits and the like. The ones who sported custom-painted helmets with the little aerodynamic wings molded into them were good for a laugh. Those were the ones who carried themselves like indoor Aytron Sennas, all surly attitude and intense posturing. Yet I never did find anyone who'd raced anywhere but at F1 Boston. And the idea of actually building, maintaining and setting up their own machines was foreign to all of them, custom helmet or no custom helmet.

In contrast, Whip City was a no-nonsense racing venue. You brought your own racecar and gear and took care of yourself. I immediately liked the place and thought about how I, too, could join in on the fun. But my interest in racing wound up taking me in another direction, because a year or two after I'd submitted my story to *Trackside* the magazine disappeared into history without so much as a whimper of warning. I, like anyone who'd contributed to the magazine as well as everyone who read it, was left stunned. Who would cover racing across the Northeast now?

Perhaps I should have left that question unanswered, but instead I decided the answer was me. Thus was born *Shorttrack Magazine*, which I created to focus on racing in New England. I hoped as well to provide a forum for the writers and photographers who'd been left in the lurch by the demise of *Trackside* as well as anyone else who wanted to give readers more to enjoy than race reports and black-and-white Victory Lane shots.

Little did I know as I began to invest every dime, hour and drop of sweat I had into my creation that it ultimately would provide me with the best racing experience my curious life ever had produced.

GOOD
STUFF

GO SPEC RACER

From Trackside Magazine, *2000. Spec cars increasingly are the way to go for most weekend warriors.*

So you start with some tired old street-beater, a Chevy Malibu, say, or maybe a Volkswagon Rabbit.

Beginning the process next to the garage, you and your buddies tear the entire interior out of the car. You pull out the seats, carpet, and headliner. You strip the doors of panels, windows and all the mechanicals that go with them. Glass gets removed, neatly if you're lucky, or in a crash of flying pieces. In place of these creature-comforts, rollcages and other safety equipment get installed, carefully and correctly, you hope.

Out comes the beater's tired old motor, replaced by a fresh powerplant you lovingly assemble from a list of junkyard or speed shop parts that have been recommended by others who promise competitive horsepower.

Finally this creation begins to resemble the racecars against which it will compete. So, after a coat of fresh paint, there's but one question remaining to be answered. Where in hell did the winter go, anyway?

There is a whiff of racefan-romance left in some of us that is energized by the image of shadetree-fabricators turning someone else's rejected ride into a trophy winner. Some old-timers cling to the concept as the definition of ``real racing.'' It goes without saying that most of these romantics never endured the process themselves. Romance is hard to find when your nose is under the fender of an old Cutlass that refuses to yield its balljoints. At that point a shadetree fabricator likely would pay a million bucks to go in the house and watch Daytona while somebody else has a fulfilling experience building them a racecar. Fortunately for them, it can cost a lot less than a million.

Today seemingly every entrepreneur who isn't losing millions in dot-commerce is introducing some new racecar. There are PRO Tour and American Race Trucks, and Legends, Mini-Cup and Baby Grand cars.

It goes without saying that a lot of people have more money than time these days. That's exactly the problem many of these one-design racers were designed to solve. All of them are serving as steps into racing for fans who otherwise would have remained in the stands or, at best, spent their capital-gains to get their names on racecars rather than their butts into them.

A lot of those butts are in Legends cars. The Legends are credited with popularizing the ``buy it and drive it'' concept, which combines two theories. The first contends that new, professionally-manufactured components designed for their application minimize the need for tuning and cobbling. The second is that if there is a minimum of fiddling allowed in the rules there will be minimal need to try.

But Greg Warzycha is one Legends driver who found that this formula hasn't always become the low-maintenance panacea originally promised.

``I love the Legends cars because they fit us perfectly,'' he says, ``but I hate the way they sell them as you just get one and go racing.

``When we got into it we got into it with the belief that everything was equal, but if you bought a brand-new car you couldn't compete.''

That likely wasn't true in the early days of the Legends, but, as with every division created to keep costs low, creeping competitiveness could not be contained. And the slippery slope of more power not only costs more money but leads to less reliability, driving costs up still further.

Some Legends racers have put as much as eight or nine-grand into the motors of cars that sell for around $12,000 new. Add components that enable these motors to make their best power at rev-ranges that exceed 11,000 RPM, bolt them into a package that weighs far more than the motorcycles the motors were designed to pull, and turn the air-cooled beasts sideways, where the back two cylinders have to fight for cooling airflow, and you better white-out the word ``bulletproof'' in your sales brochure.

That's what Mark Piekarski learned when he started looking to move his son B. J. beyond race karts and mini-cuppers into the world of coil-over suspension and free-choice among chassis-setup options. The Piekarskis were looking hard at Legends, but the more they looked the harder it became to gaze beyond the full-bodied, racing-slicked Baby Grands.

``I kept my ear to the ground,'' recalls the elder Piekarski, ``and I just kept hearing raves about these cars. People were saying `That's the one I change the oil and park in the corner.' So I guess the main thing was the low maintenance.''

By any estimation the Baby Grands are every bit the serious racecars Legends are. Although cloaked in pseudo-Winston Cup bodies, these cars are truer to junior Pro Stocks than junior Cup cars. And the mig-welded, coilover suspended chassis is stoutly-engineered and fitted with first-class components.

Indeed, Piekarski liked the product so much he joined the sales force. As Motorsports of New England, he's become regional distributor for Baby Grand Manufacturing.

Thanks to Piekarski's efforts they have a track to race the Baby Grands. After much persuasion Piekarski reached agreement with Seekonk Speedway to host a season of Baby Grand racing. Not that it was an easy sell when Speedway director Francis Venditti was approached.

``He hemmed and hawed,'' explains Piekarski, ``and finally let us come and run a couple of laps on a Sunday when they were running enduros. Then we put it (on display) during his Labor Day show. You would have thought it was a Winston Cup car.''

That was enough to convince Venditti that this was a growing series.

Jim Langevin and Joe Harkins would like to believe that they've created a growing series as well, but the growth has been slow for their Turn-Two Modifieds. That's a shame, because for racers who do their homework theirs might be the best deal of all.

The concept of the T-2 Mods is similiar to those of the Legends and Baby Grands, but their differences are noteworthy. Where the former two cars run air-cooled Yamaha motors the T-2's utilize power made by water-cooled Suzuki powerplants, a unit better-suited to the north-south configuration of the typical stock car. And the three-link rear suspension and other specs of the T-2 probably better prepare racers for what they can expect if they move into higher divisions.

There also is an honesty about the appearance of the T-2 Mods that is appreciated by those who approach racing with no pretense. They don't look like Winston Cup cars, or coupes that raced decades ago. They look like modifieds look and occupy a place in the mod spectrum only a tick below a Pro Four Mod, a car for which they easily can be mistaken, even by seasoned race watchers.

Unlike the Pro Fours, though, there's no room for improvisation with a Turn-Two Mod. Every car must run the same Suzuki motor and internal components must be from the Suzuki parts book.

``We don't want guys buying speed," Langevin declares. ``If you're going to go faster you're going to do it driving."

Langevin and Harkins don't have the resources of other car builders, but the car they build is every bit the quality piece a Legends or Baby Grand car is. In fact a Turn-Two Mod may be a stouter car, not only than those two but than even a Pro Four. The fact that they build them locally also can be advantageous. ``We just sold a car to one guy who came here, got into the car

while we scaled it and then loaded it on his truck," Langevin recalls. ``Three days later he was at the track and ready to go racing."

The track was Londonderry Raceway. It serves as home for the T-2 Mods, and it's a good one, with a quarter-mile of smooth, high-banked pavement.

Last season the division also raced at Monadnock, Claremont and Riverside and would like to continue to travel. But the division needs more cars if it really wants to grow. Which can work for prospective customers, of course.

``If somebody wants a car we'll give up ours," he states Harkins and himself. Or you could run one of theirs while they put yours together.

Maybe, though, you're more of a traditionalist. You don't want to build a V-8 in your garage, but you still want one under your hood. In that case an American Race Truck might be more your ticket into the show.

Then you'll want to contact Tom Fox. The SK Modified racer also sells the Arizona-built ART trucks for a series that runs primarily at Waterford Speedbowl. These machines would make most street or strictly stock drivers feel right at home, with the aforementioned small-block motors bolted into a massaged version of General Motors' metric chassis, the favorite among street stock racers who don't compete at Seekonk.

Onto this platform ART bolts a fibreglass pickup body and associated racecar bits. The result is a full-size racecar (er...truck) that nonetheless shares much of the philosophy of its smaller cousins as well as a price of under $15,000.

As with all of these spec racers the formula forces competitors to find speed through better handling.

``There are plenty of adjustments you can make to make them faster,'' says Fox. ``There's a lot of fun a lot of guys can have with about a dozen adjustments.''

That's what makes all of these racers so great. Everybody has tools. It's nice when you can use them to go faster without having to buy something to bolt on first.

There are other bennies for American Race Truckers. Most of these series offer some level of touring, and some times in creative ways. Fox almost put together a weekend that would have been a fantastic experience for any ART competitor.

``We had made a deal to do a Friday/Saturday visit to Canaan,'' he related. ``We were going to run a dirt/pavement weekend. The guys seemed real excited about it.''

Unfortunately Canaan's pavement operation shut down, but the deal still serves to illustrate what these series offer to racers and fans alike.

``The tracks are looking for new ideas,'' Langevin points out, ``and they want cars that are cheap to run. If the cars are cheap to run they don't have to pay as much in purses.''

Good-looking cars. Close, exciting racing. Victories earned on the track, not at the bank. Sounds like ``real racing'' to me.

SPORT TRUCKS

This appeared in Trackside Magazine *in 2001. The sport trucks still race at Seekonk, although they now can run V-8s.*

Every racetrack has its path to glory. Usually that path starts with some tired old hulk getting dragged out of a field or from behind the garage. Then it gets made relatively safe, is stripped of every pound not essential to its mission, and is massaged more lovingly than it deserves to be into some sort of ragged racecar.

It's called a street stock, or strictly stock, or rookie or hobby or mini stock. Or it gets called something sillier – roadrunner springs to mind as one example.

If you're lucky, and good, your path in that car will climb up toward the glory of a late model, pro stock or some sort of modified, maybe super, maybe not. But once you've buckled in to one of these sleek thoroughbreds you know you're on your way. Unless, of course, glory is not where you want your path to go. Free of that imperative, you get to choose a different path. And suddenly you notice that there are many you can take. So you step off that crowded path to racing glory and onto one that suits you better.

Not as many racetracks have such paths. Too many divisions are created and groomed to serve as primers to aspiring would-be racing stars. Too few are created just to be a ball to compete in, future pro stock car-counts be damned.

When it comes to truck divisions motives become even more clouded. Promoters point to what's parked in the lots surrounding their tracks and speak of ``brand identity'' as if they're selling trucks, not racing. They write rules that echo those of the cars that race at their tracks and then wonder why nobody wants to build a late model with a fleetside pick-up bed.

The people at Seekonk Speedway might tell you they created a truck division with both paths in mind. And they might be right. The path to glory at Seekonk might take you right through their Sport Truck division. Another path, though, might stop right there. You might call it the path to a plain old good time.

The beauty of the sport trucks, and the key to why they've become such unique and popular attractions, may come from the fact that, unlike most of the pick-up divisions that have struggled at New England shorttracks, they actually predate NASCAR's market-driven Craftsman Truck Series. They also were born in the middle of a traditional racing ritual, the post-race rap session.

``We had a tech man, Ed Morin, who had a Ford Ranger,'' recalls the speedway's chief tech inspector, Dave Alburn. ``It was a little hopped up. We were standing around it one night after the racing was done, and we got to talking. That's where the idea came from.''

If you know anything about Ford's Ranger pick-up you understand or at least suspect another important point about Seekonk's sports trucks. Unlike almost every truck division ever created, sport trucks are compact pick-ups that run with four-cylinder power.

``We wanted to put a division together a little above a street stock but below a sportsman,'' explains Alburn. ``We figured 'Why not a division for four cylinders?' ''

Already Seekonk had one of those, its almost below entry-level Formula Fours, which utilized bone-stock econoboxes and other subcompacts. But here the idea was to combine low cost with the more conventional parameters of oval-track racing, namely engines that don't barrel down the racetrack sideways, and power directed to wheels pushing, not pulling, their way to the checkered flag. Viewed from that perspective, Ford Rangers and Chevy S-10s made perfect sense. Not to mention Toyotas and a few other brands not usually tooling around ovals.

``They were inexpensive, but you could use your own ideas,'' says Alburn. ``You had to. They weren't built for racing so you had to think things out for yourself.''

That proved to be the initial attraction for the first competitors to get involved in the division.

``Billy Clarke had a big part in it,'' Alburn says. ``Also a gentleman named Joe Putnam. He's a very smart guy and likes to tinker around, and he got into it.''

A tireless, even obsessed tinkerer himself, Clarke tore into the first truck to be called, well, not sport truck, but ``TD-4,'' the division's first, awkward moniker. His truck would serve as the division's prototype.

``We were trying to keep it kind of stock,'' remembers Clarke, an ageless Seekonk veteran who amazingly is now in his sixth decade of competition. But keeping Clarke's Ranger-based creation stock proved tough.

``There was no way you could use the stock Ford front-end,'' admits Clarke of Ford's twin I-beam confiuration. ``I tried for weeks to make it work.''

Ultimately Clarke used spherical rod-ends to provide some set-up room.

``You could adjust them all over the place,'' Clarke concludes.

But the process of arriving at this solution came to illustrate the ongoing process of writing rules that combined stock cast-off pieces with racing parts that would keep prices down in the long run. Speedway officials typically weighed in toward the stock end of the spectrum. Clarke, ever the seeker of an edge, took a broader view. Another example came to light as the track's planners maintained that bores should remain strictly to stock specs, even if that required resleeving old motors bored by owners looking to extend the lives of tired trucks.

``I said `Nobody's going to do that,' '' Clarke relates. ``Just let em bore em out - 030 - 060. Who cares?''

The imput of Clarke, Putnam and the few other drivers who put together TD-4s that first season helped the trucks evolve into real

36

attractive rides. And Clarke, for one, couldn't keep his hands off his creations, ripping them apart and rebuilding often to try different ideas. As one example, he finally tore out the twin I-beams in favor of the more conventional front end from a Mustang II.

The changes have worked, and Clarke has stayed near the front of an ever-expanding pack of trucks. Last season, in fact, Clarke finished second in the sport truck championship. The fact that he didn't win the title is his own fault, at least as far as the actual champion is concerned.

``You're building another one?" Brian Clarke recalls asking his father. ``I'm building one for you," was his father's reply.

Brian had raced years ago before marriage, kids and all the trappings of a real life came along to get in the way. But in a sport truck the younger Clarke has found that, save for the pressure that any points-race creates to tow to the track every week, his racing actually has left enough room for other pursuits important to him. His championship season is a testament to that.

``I planned to take last year off," he says. "My father kept pestering me."

Finally, ``It was the Friday night before the Sunday Seekonk opened. I said 'To shut you up I'll get the truck ready.' I'd put anti-freeze in it and parked it behind the barn. I flushed out the radiator and put a battery in it and set the toe – I'd tapped somebody in the (final race) the year before – and went out and finished third."

Clarke didn't decide to go crazy based on his first-week success. It was more like just the opposite.

``I took the attitude I'm not going to spend five nights a week in the garage," Clarke says, and he stuck to his declaration. And this while chasing a title with a four year-old engine.

``He took it out in practice the last race and said 'I don't think it's going to make it," the elder Clarke muses. ``He told me 'It's got only 25 pounds of pressure.' I said ``That's good enough.' He won the feature in it."

Don't dismiss Clarke's success because the sport trucks are off the beaten path. They've proven there are plenty of talented drivers who want to travel the road less taken. Some of them have chased the glory, captured it even. In addition to the elder Clarke Seekonk champion

Johnnie Tripp has been a regular sport truck competitor. So has past Pro-Four titlist Joe Lemay. Former Pro Stock regular George Rego has found a comfortable home in a sport truck, as has Sportsman driver Steve Taylor.

The chance to run against these vets is one thing that interested sport truck vet Robin Sloane when she looked to move up from the Formula-Fours.

``The appeal was there were quite a few people with experience you could race with," she agrees, ``and it still was going to be inexpensive."

It helped that Sloane had run a Mustang in the F-4 division and was able to transfer many components from her car to her truck. But there was a more important attraction than low expense. Sloane also liked the idea that there was room for innovation.

``It wasn't like you had 40 street stocks out there that were all Camaros," she says. ``You''ll find that we're all going down the same road, but we all think there's one thing better than the other along the lines of a different cam, or there's a lot of different heads you can use.

``Like I like a car that's really soft. I don't think I could drive a car that's real stiff, but some guys like them that way."

Still, Sloane has valued the opportunity to learn against drivers who have a lot to teach. Another former pro stocker who turned some laps in a sport truck reinforced that value to her.

``Norm Holden said to me one time 'If you can get around the track with the equipment you have now you'll do fine. It's just a matter of reacclimating yourself to the higher speed.' "

Maybe that's why another Seekonk Speedway pro stock champion, Vinnie Annarummo, steered his son into a sport truck when he entered racing.

``There's more people who know what they're doing," he declares. ``There's not a lot of banging. There's a lot of racing."

Annarummo also feels there's value for a driver who is hoping to take the walk toward a pro stock or other racing exotica.

``The set-up's basically the same," he maintains. ``It's a little lighter, but you still shock it the same way you do a normal car.''

Todd Annarummo has proven a fast learner. He provided the ongoing input to a truck that won three races in his rookie season.

``He asked `How should I set the springs up,' " says Vinnie. ``He started with that, but he's made the changes himself since then."

Chances are Annarummo the younger will look to move up as soon as he can convince his father to let him. When he does he won't find the camaraderie and support he's enjoyed in his sport truck. That's another feature that keeps many sport truck drivers content to stay where they are. It's been that way from the beginning.

``Nobody knew how it was going to go so they all worked together," relates Alburn. ``The Fords, nobody knew how they'd work so those guys worked together. The Chevies, some were staying together some weren't. So they were close."

Most still are. Oh, it's racing, so beefs do spring up. But when you consider a competitor a friend you're more likely to listen when you meet in the pits after the race. And if you know you've been having a good time racing you're more likely to want to keep it that way. Smiles won't get you into a pro stock if you're on your way to glory. But a pro stock won't get you many smiles if it's a good time you're looking for.

``As long as you're all teeth and all smiles," says Sloane with a chuckle, ``you're having a good time."

There's only so much glory to be found at a racetrack. In the sport trucks a good time can be had by all.

GOOD TIMES – NOT!

From Shorttrack Magazine, *2005. It wasn't really that bad. I never did make it to Spud, though.*

Yeah, I know all about, "In like a lion. Out like a lamb." I know the first day of spring comes in March. I don't care. I hate the month.

I hate it because it picks at you, like snotty kids trying to aggravate you, knowing they can get away with it, and there's nothing you can do about it. I hate it because it teases you, offering hints at the rebirth of everything, only to rub your face in it, "it" being piles of snow as deep as any all winter.

I hate how dead everything remains, with any charm the snow might render long-gone under thick slogs of mud. March reminds you of everything that's coming but gives you none of it.

Oh, yeah, and I hate basketball.

Yes, I know March has disappeared into the rearview by now. As you read this it very well could be a beautifully balmy day, with blossoms exploding and our first races of the year roaring around the track. I don't care. Where I'm sitting, sleet is crashing against the window and mocking anyone foolish enough to think "It's almost Spring."

Normally l keep these feelings to myself (Okay, my wife has to deal with them, but she's such an angel, aren't you, Dear?). This, however, has turned out to be one of the all-time worst Marches of my life. Bad enough the furnace has a leak in it. It took me two months to get an estimate to repair the gasket for the tankless water-heater that turned out to be the price to replace the entire furnace.

You'll love this. The oil company's service manager told me, "You can't get that bolt out. That's a steel bolt in a cast-iron tank."

I'm contemplating doing the job myself. I have a torch. Guess he doesn't.

I held off, though, after the molar started driving me crazy. Actually I was holding off on that, too, but the pain got me to the point of insanity, making waste of a week before I got to the dentist to hear the official diagnosis: "Absess." After that it took another week or so for the antibiotics to kick in.

Of course, I had to cancel the appointment for the root canal. I was too miserable with the flu to pick my head up off the pillow to do anything but... well, you know what.

All this time lying around feeling miserable gave me plenty of time to think, though. As well as serious motivation to focus on something more pleasant than what I was experiencing. I've been thinking a lot, then, with much of it pretty unfocused on anything ("Wow! 1 remember hallucinations!") but at least a little of it focused with great effort on what I want to be doing once I can stand more than three or four minutes without drifting into the shower-stall.

I spent the winter maintaining a pretty steady supply of optimism for the coming shorttrack season. I saw that many tracks had taken assertive steps to enhance their weekly divisions. New entry-level classes offer attractions for undercards while some tracks have really stepped forward with their headliners. I mean, there are weekly mods at a bunch of tracks!

You can see touring mods race in every state in New England, save for Rhode Island, where the only things racing are the hearts of slots players at Newport Grande. Except that recently the state was featured in national-stage rumors as the one kingdom that Ken Schrader, that Fast Man of La Mancha, still hopes to conquer.

Midgets are strong. Not just NEMA's classics but in "lite" versions that might offer the thrill of a lifetime for many would-be open-wheelers.

41

There's even going to be an asphalt/dirt "home-and-home" winged/wingless weekend series for those low-budget"lite" cars.

I am determined that this year I will wipe the last three tracks in New England off my list of venues yet to be visited; y'up, even Spud. I went to All-Star twice last year and enjoyed the rainouts. I will be there this year when the supers are. I hope some supers will be there, too. With more ISMA events in the Midwest than in New England and gas at about 20 bucks a gallon by summer, I still bet there'll be a few.

There's a bunch of places to go, a bunch of races to see. Sure, gas is expensive, but skip that week you planned at some far-flung locale. A three-hour drive to a different racetrack isn't so hard to digest. Look at me. I'm eating solid foods again. I must be getting better.

Now to call about the root canal.

Sigh.

MY FAVORITE RACE

From Trackside Magazine*, 1993. The best race I've ever witnessed – even decades later.*

Yankees never are thrilled with the prospect of a British invasion. They didn't like the first one. Many weren't thrilled with the musical one 200 years later. And seven years ago, when Formula One's reigning World Champion Nigel Mansell invaded these shores to compete in CART's PPG Indy Car World Series, they they weren't too happy, either.

Mansell didn't endear himself to anyone when he launched himself in the New World like an intercontinental missile, taking the pole and then racing to the win in the CART season-opener at Surfer's Paradise in Australia. Nobody was impressed with his British charm when he immediately established himself as the man to beat in the series almost before the K-Mart and Havoline colors had dried on his Newman/Haas Lola-Ford.

Add to that the comparisons to the less-than-impressive debut in Formula One of the man he replaced at Newman/Haas, Michael Andretti, and the new season dawned dark indeed for stateside fans that spring.

It was only the beginning. Mansell was on his way to five wins, seven poles and a history-making season as the first rookie ever to win an Indy car championship. He also was in the midst of proving he was one road racer who could find the fast way around an oval track. But if the massively-egoed Mansell was not surprised by his oval-track success by the time CART descended on New Hampshire International Speedway, the success he enjoyed on the long straights and flat turns that made up the mile or so of NHIS asphalt would surprise him for a different and infinitely better reason.

As August dawned and CART's teams headed to Roger Penske's Michigan International Speedway Mansell actually trailed Penske pilot Emerson Fittipaldi, himself a former world champ, by three points in the race for the title. Fittipaldi had taken the lead after CART's race through the fairgrounds of the Canadian National Exposition in Toronto. In the title-hunt as well was Penske's new driver, Paul Tracy, who'd been hired to fill the seat left open with the retirement of Rick Mears.

Tracy also was working on his now ironclad reputation for spectacular inconsistency. He'd won at Toronto, and also at Cleveland. Yet at Phoenix, for just one example, he'd spun out of the lead despite an amazing two-lap margin over the rest of the field. Mansell's teammate Mario Andretti had inherited that win, his last ever in an Indy car.

Such was the dominance in the series of these two teams that a win at Detroit by Danny Sullivan was the only blemish on the string of victories they shared.

At NHIS, though, the focus was back on Newman/Haas after Mansell won the week before at Michigan. Fans stood five-deep at the back of the team's trailer hoping to get a glimpse of the team's drivers as they hid up front. When Mansell did come out of hiding a crowd would swarm around him, moving with the star of the moment the way a horde of Winston Cup fans moves as a mass when Jeff Gordon forms its nucleus. Amidst this attention Mansell charmed everyone with a display of grace at odds with the reputation for bitchiness he'd brought with him from Europe. It was easy to believe, though, that Mansell's demeanor was not an act, for the level of tension in the air at NHIS was closer to what one might expect at a vintage racing outing than what Mansell had endured chasing the Formula One circus.

The press, too, was charmed by Mansell. He seemed to make all the right remarks, praising his CART competitors and complimenting the Bahres for the professionalism of their still-young facility and operation.

The media, at least those members not reflexively smitten by the simple fact of the Winston Cup's recent NHIS debut, ate it up. Here in its face was a real story, not to mention the potential for a world-class competition among world-class athletes.

As the weekend unfolded the focus of everyone on the 200-lap CART race grew more intense. For one thing, Saturday's slate of support races, which included Formula Atlantic's only New Hampshire visit and an incongruous Busch North date, provided little excitement. But it would not have mattered if the modifieds had been on-hand to produce their traditional 40 laps of scream-inducing intensity. On this weekend the Indy cars would not be upstaged. Nigel Mansell would see to that.

The race started with Mansell on the pole flanked by an unlikely front-row partner in Raul Boesel. Al Unser, Jr., soon to move to Penske but then as now driving for Rick Galles, lined up inside Emmo and behind Mansell. Behind them was a field filled with top open-wheel drivers, including then-champion Bobby Rahal, Jimmy Vasser, Teo Fabi, Arie Luyendyk and Scott Goodyear. They'd qualified closer together than any Indy car field before them, foreshadowing the race to come.

Mired in the middle of the pack was Tracy, but in his typical fashion he charged toward the front. Soon the first of many battles between him and Mansell was unfolding before a respectable race-day crowd. Fittipaldi, too, took his turns challenging for the lead. But Tracy quickly moved into first, dogged by the British champion.

Others dropped from contention. Andretti found the wall – and Goodyear – retiring both for the day. Boesel did the same. By then, though, it already was clear that this was a three-car race. Tracy continued to lead, but this was no Phoenix. He was unable to open a comfortable gap.

Even as pit cycles were completed Tracy, Mansell and Fittipaldi were never long away from the front of the field. Fittipaldi, for one, pitted early out-of-cycle, yet with his car adjusted and otherwise rejuvenated, he roared back into the lead pack within 15 laps.

Yellow flags came, but the passing was taking place on the track. And once the green flag fell on lap-156, after the mess made by Andretti and Goodyear was cleaned up, the yellow was never seen again.

Now Mansell was making his last charge at Tracy, who'd led from lap-95. Finally, with ten laps to go, their two cars were nose-to-tail, with Fittipaldi close behind. The final chase was on.

Anyone viewing Paul Tracy's attempts to use slower traffic to hold off Mansell would have agreed that it was some of the smartest driving Tracy ever demonstrated. They might have thought it should have been more than enough to get the job done. But Nigel Mansell was exhibiting a level of nerve and resolve that had everyone holding their breath as they watched the battle before them. More than once Mansell followed Tracy around a lapped car and found room behind him where it seemed none existed. There was no chance that Fittipaldi could stay in this hunt.

Tracy later would claim that his Penske was the strongest of the three contending cars when all carried heavy loads, but that as fuel was burned off the edge shifted to his two opponents. That might have been true, but it could not tarnish the lustre of the move Mansell made with three laps left in the race. As the leaders flew through turn-two and headed for the back straight Mansell charged to the outside and, seemingly through sheer force of will, edged past Tracy to take a lead that Tracy could not overcome. Mansell flew under the checkered flag with a winning margin of less than half-a-second.

In the post-race press conference, Tracy displayed a level of class not always apparent in later years.

``I think it was one of the best races of the year," he declared. ``Those last ten laps were white-knuckle, let's-get-it-on racing. It was serious racing."

Mansell, who'd just given himself an unmatchable 40th birthday present, waxed even more enthusiastically.

``I learned some moves from Emerson and Paul I didn't even know about. And this racing on short ovals is the best racing there is. I've been side-by-side at 200 miles-per, but that was nothing compared to racing here today.

``I found out that we could race all sorts of different lines," he continued. ``And you had to think of what everyone else was doing, whether it was Paul or Emerson or the traffic we were in. I take my hat off to every driver out there. It takes incredible discipline from every driver to do what we did. This is thoroughbred racing. I've never experienced anything like it. This is very refreshing."

Unfortunately Mansell could not retain that feeling of wonder the following season as he unsuccessfully defended his championship. The frustration of the '94 season revealed the side of Mansell of which McLaren, his last Formula One employer, and the rest of the F-1 family had tired. Before even that point, though, many were questioning Mansell's sincerity in enthusing over that day in New Hampshire.

But read ``Nigel Mansell; My Autobiography,'' and refer to an appendix that lists Mansell's choices as his ten greatest races. There, among the descriptions of landmarks in his path to world-championships, you'll find listed ``Loudon, NH, August 8, 1993.''

``Old-time American racers came up to me afterwards,'' he wrote, ``and told me it was one of the best races they'd ever seen. It was brilliant, pure racing.''

That is something any racefan can appreciate. And it's something that any real racefan in attendance that day at Loudon most assuredly still savors to this day.

MY FAVORITE THINGS

From Trackside Magazine, *2001. If you count them it's supposed to be 1,000 words; you know, what one picture is worth.*

Since I wrote this, a few of my favorite folks are gone or gone from racing, as are some tracks, series and racecars.

But they're still all my favorites.

Open-rule pro stock races; the Icebreaker; the Icebreaker being back; modifieds; Dale Eamhardt flags hanging on houses in neighborhoods filled with houses flying ladybug flags; karting; the Wood Brothers (the super drivers, not the Winston Cup team); modifieds wheel-to-wheel at NHIS; "Acres of Free Parking"; women right out there competing with men; any woman who does it; roadrunners wheel to wheel at HIS; Dave Dion; midgets; doughboys; green-white-checkereds; Ted Christopher; Whip City; hard-charger awards; exhausts glowing "on-fire" red; "creative engineering" (nudge-nudge, wink-wink); Carl Tirone; the Indy 500, "The Greatest Spectacle in Racing!"; visits to R. A.'s; the Webbers; the fact that racing's biggest stars generally aren't #*&#*#% jerks; the Pasteryaks; bench racing; cars at every racetrack painted to look like Jeff Gordon's; the Balsers.

The Pines, open or closed; The Wood Brothers, (the Cup team, not the super drivers); Ted Christopher; midgets on pavement; Ray Belanger; the

Milk Bowl; supermods at Seekonk; the continual class of Brad Leighton; almost looping the D&D Super at Canaan while moving about as fast as Joey Payne gets pushed through the pits; busy race shops in the dead of night; Chris Beaudry's dad saying, "He's been reading your column since he was 12."; cool paint schemes; stop-and-goes; Rick Martin; dirt tracks; Ted Christopher; "The Unpredictable Hobby Stocks"; Dion off-line and passing people; Monadnock's doughboys, which are the size of sewer covers; childhood-memories of standing in my grandmother's front yard listening to the sounds of racing from Seekonk Speedway; recently standing in my front yard listening to the sounds of racing from Thompson Speedway; the old wooden grandstands at Canaan; the Franboni; just about every NEMA driver I've ever talked to; Lou Modestino's TV calender; the fact that half the town of Westport, Mass., seems to drive a racecar at Seekonk Speedway; Bob Bahre; Bob Potter; "turn right to go left"; White Mountain Motorsports Park; Bobby Gahan; slot cars; midgets on dirt; NEAR; memories of racing with Dave; Bob Nolet's ability to smile through anything; long phone calls at work that "are not work-related,"; coupes; Ted Christopher; coupes still racing up North; midgets at Seekonk; sitting at the campsite at NHIS reading the same story over and over as published in every trade paper given out in the media room; seeing Walt Renner still at it; Ed Flemke Jr.'s attitude; my first win in a kart at Pomfret; my second win in a kart at Pomfret; my fourth-place finish in a kart at the Woodstock Fair, which still was more fun than either win; roadsters.

Kyle Petty; biplanes landing over Whip City as the sun sets; old Monte Carlos turned into street stocks; driving the race truck home in the middle of the night; first-time winners; old-timers getting just one more win; running into Tom Neff; Jeff Gordon (yeah – Jeff Gordon); old racetracks; Bob Webber's opinions on anything, even when I don't agree with him; Ted Christopher; Bill Clarke's Henry J-bodied.coupe; riding the cushion; Turn-Two Modifieds; Speedvision; "They touch!"

James Hylton showing up for the first Winston Cup race at NHIS, his car on an open trailer pulled by a clapped-out utility truck; slower traffic on the track; .slower traffic on the highway heading home; getting paid to talk about racing, which of course is a whole lot easier than doing it; drivers going 150 laps on the same set of tires at Stafford – and winning;

new racetracks; expressway-wide corners at Beech Ridge; Walt Scadden's quad-4 midget.

Waterford's mini stocks, which almost exclusively are Ford Mustangs built up in classic street-stock style; Ted Christopher; Hampton Inn-ternational Speedway; coaches; in-out boxes; wingless Sprinters; Pete Fiandaca; the infield at Daytona; stopping at a diner on the way a – real diner; Paul Dunigan; A-J (any of them); consis; getting hit by clods of mud at a dirt track, rubber at a paved track;

Brad Whitford of Aerosmith driving an Indy Lights car at NHIS (he sucked); Dr. Jack Miller, "The Racing Dentist," passing out toothbrushes before driving his Indy Lights car at NHIS (he sucked, too); Nigel Mansell driving an Indy car at NHIS (he did not suck); Ted Christopher; actually finding Bear Ridge; Dale Shaw running up through the field; the sound of midgets screaming around the track; the sound of modifieds roaring around the track; a grid full of pristine racecars on opening night; Ray Lee's low-buck pro stock; a racecar in an open garage; four-wheel drifts; Dick Trickle, in his driving suit, working on his Winston Cup car; somebody making a pass on the inside going into turn one, only to get passed on the inside coming out of turn two by the driver he just got by; that smell; a grid full of wrinkled race cars on the last race day of the season; Ted Christopher; Vinnie Who?; Pete Zanardi, and his brother Alex; the Oxford 250 , although it's been better; a bad day at the races, which still is better than a good day almost anywhere else (unless you're racing. Then it's worse than you can imagine); Russ Dowd's sonorous voice booming over the Thompson P.A. system; Tom Carnegie likewise booming "It's a new track record!"; flat out through the corner the first time you do it; open wheels; watching somebody go from last to first; Ted Christopher; tear-offs sparkling as they float to the track under the lights; pulling into the pits on race day;.'60s Indy cars; posing with the checkered flag; photo-finishes;

"Racing every Saturday Night!" Jim Hurtubise refusing to give it up; drivers so excited by a win they forget their sponsors; Eddie Cheever; George Savary, although it's time he moved on; *Trackside*.

Did I mention Ted Christopher?

NHIS: BUILT FOR OPEN WHEELS

From Trackside Magazine, *2003*

So Winston Cup races come and go up at New Hampshire International Speedway, and after the Cup caravan heads south we're all left to ponder what sort of race we witnessed.

Sometimes, such as this past July, the race turns out to be a passable spectacle, as in somebody was able to pass somebody. Sometimes the only passing of any consequence comes as teams make their way out of town, where they're passing anything they can put behind them in an effort to put spatial as well as emotional distance between themselves and the painful memories of racing on the Black-Magic Mile. This usually comes despite some latest mega-dollar modification to the place Bob Bahre has rendered in his quest to keep the petulant Cup drivers happy, since paying them more for their toils than any track save Daytona hasn't seemed to be enough. But there are some mods that leave no room for debate. Hey, with those mods there isn't enough room for the thickness of the paper these words are printed on to be slipped between them.

Nobody has to discuss whether these mods, which are not made to the track but rather perform on it, manage to give meaning to the term ``Magic Mile." But instead (since for one thing this is *Trackside's*

Modifieds Issue) it might be interesting to discuss just why the best race of every Winston Cup weekend at NHIS always has to come on Friday, before most fans have bought their beer for the weekend.

I've always felt that the lousy Cup races at NHIS were more a factor of lousy cars than it was a lousy racetrack. I've never heard any Cup driver, mechanic, official or even reporter utter a comment to that effect, but I have often, nonetheless. The evidence comes every July and September. Cup and Busch cars are Exhibit A, Modifieds are Exhibit B (Indy Cars are Exhibit C, but that's an issue for another – um – issue).

Why is this so? It's easy to identify technical factors in favor of the mods, such as lower weight, higher horsepower, wider tires, better brakes and such. But is that all there is to it? These two types of cars might be far from equal but they're at least equal to the cars they're racing against. How can three, four, or even five mods race for the lead lap after lap looking as if they're welded together while two Cup cars look like the same poles on two magnets when they have a chance to go at each other?

The easy answers can be found in the tech articles. If there's more to the story that could only come from the driver's seats of both types of cars. But there aren't too many drivers who've driven both types of cars at New Hampshire, perhaps none who've raced both Cup cars and Mods there. The closest I could get was to talk to a couple of drivers who race both mods and Busch North cars there regularly. No matter. As far as I'm concerned both Mike Stefanik and Ted Christopher would acquit themselves well if given a real chance to run in the Winston Cup Series. Besides, they'd both be more fun to talk to than the Jeff Gordons of Winston Cup even if Gordon was on a bender.

First of all, Christopher wants to make one point about racing taxi-cabs at NHIS.

``I started 43rd in my taxi-cab and I won," he points out, "so you *can* pass there."

Then he identifies another technical factor, one foisted upon the mods so they wouldn't be overheating stop watches and making the Winston Cup cars look even worse.

``Maybe with the restrictor plates (required at NHIS) it keeps us together."

``It's easier to drive," Stefanik agrees. ``We're going as fast on the corners as we are on the straights, so there's no significant acceleration. And with the `dirtiness' of the cars and their drag, it's hard to get away from other cars."

``A full-fendered car to me needs the banks. You need compression on the inside tires to get some bite so you can really drive."

Yeah, yeah. More technical stuff. But keep these guys talking. You'll start to get to the bottom of the story.

``Maybe we're just used to running side by side (there)," says Christopher. ``It is fun to run there. Any place that's fast is fun."

``The modifieds are fun to drive on a flat track because they're so light and you have so much tire you still get the bite," says Stefanik. ``So you can drive it anywhere. It's just more fun."

``Mods are more fun on any track. They're just so much fun to drive. If you're not having fun driving a modified you need to rethink why you're racing."

Fun. Yes. The last guy I saw having fun driving a Cup car was Juan Pablo Montoya.

``I think," says Christopher, mostly seriously, in conclusion, ``we're more racers, not just riders."

Of course, around here we already know that. If you don't, it's not too late to get September 12 off.

What Makes
A Good Track Good?

From Trackside Magazine, *1996. These guys have all retired now, but what they said about these tracks – and tracks in general – still applies.*

D id you happen to catch the Busch race a couple of months ago at the new Homestead Racing Complex down in southern Florida? CBS, which broadcast the race, devoted plenty of time to lavish praise of the stylish new facility, with its superspeedway-layout embellished by art deco color and detail. The place truly is a wonder of wonders, at home in a region where the honest, straightforward and workable are ignored in favor of flash.

Yet there were the drivers, the people who were paid to make the place come alive, referring to it as a one-groove circuit that provided little room for passing unless you wanted to banzai it into a corner and scare the art deco out of everyone with a dive under a braking competitor.

How did this happen? How do you end up building a Taj Mahal only to have it surround a track that seemingly is as exciting as a vegetable garden?

And Homestead is hardly the only racetrack with this problem. There are plenty of tracks, relatively new ones, that seem to inspire less-than-exciting racing. On the other hand, there is many a grizzled old dog of a racetrack that just seems to bring out the best in the drivers who are busy cursing the place.

What makes the difference? What is it that makes a great racetrack? Is there a formula that these racetrack builders should be using to avoid making an expensive mistake? And is it too late once a track has been built to make it a better one? Is there hope for Homestead?

Don't ask me. From the stands or the press box, it's the drivers who make a great racetrack because it's the drivers who make a great race. So ask the drivers. What do they look for? What brings out the best in them?

"A good racetrack is a track that's easy to pass on,' states midget driver and NEMA honcho Bobby Seymour simply. "For instance," he continues, "Seekonk is an ideal midget track. You can start in the back, and all of a sudden you're at the front."

What is it about Seekonk that's so special?

"It's wide, with short straights and wide, sweeping corners with some banking," says Seymour. "It's not a circle, but it's almost one. You can carry a lot of speed into the corners and you can use the whole track. That's when you'll see a lot of passing."

Russ Wood sees things a little differently from the seat of his Auto Palace supermodified. A little more horsepower evidently changes a driver's perspective.

"I prefer something with heavily-banked turns and long straights," he says. "I really like Thompson. It just has a better feeling driving into a banked turn. And in and out of the turn, you've got a couple of different lines.

"I like going fast there. You'll get a lot of passing on those straights."

Passing on a straight may be exciting to race watchers, but Dave Dion, for one, doesn't think it's necessarily a reflection of driving skill.

"If you're not rich, it's bad," he claims. "On a track like that, you need horsepower and you need state-of-the-art high-tech brakes. Shorter tracks are handling tracks. You have to work on a handling track. Handling comes from learning. It's something money can't buy.

"You don't have to have any money at Seekonk" Dion continues. "You just have to keep your head on straight. It's a great little track. You can never blame anybody for beating you with money there."

But Dion would say the same about Thompson.

"Funny thing is you could spot a guy 50 horsepower at Thompson. It's got a lot of banking so you can use every groove on the track."

To better illustrate his point, Dion mentions the ultimate example of racetrack banking.

"Go to Daytona. You'll see that some guys are up in the Speedi-Dri and other guys are on the apron."

Seymour sees things differently.

"I don't think you need a Winchester or a Daytona to have good passing," he says. "You can have too much banking and cars can get so hooked up it gets harder to pass. And you can have a very flat track if you get the layout right. Beech Ridge and Oxford are almost flat, but they're wide with sweeping turns and lots of run-off room."

What do all these tracks have in common? Let Mike Weeden, who won Pro Stock championships at Thompson as well as Star and Lee this year, sum it up.

"The most important feature when you look at a racetrack is side-by-side racing" he declares. "For that you have to have two grooves that work

"A lot of tracks have a groove and a half. You can pass, but a lot of guys don't want to get out there."

Weeden mentions the usual suspects in explaining what makes a track work, but he adds one more.

"The physical configuration is important," he says, "but the management of a track is, too."

How can management affect how well a track works?

"Sometimes when you get outside, there are guys who try to take it away," he claims. "I won't mince words. At Star Speedway, some of those guys get out there, and they won't let you use the outside.

"You have to have – call it a code of honor. When you get beyond a certain point, you have to let a guy go. The management has to control that, or it turns into slam-bang racing."

"Star is tough," Wood admits. "You don't have a heck of a lot of room there. It's changed a lot over the years. The bottom groove has pretty much disappeared. I think enduro (cars) have a lot to do with that. When they first had the enduros, there were 100 cars out there, and every one of them was leaking oil or anti-freeze. We got out there and we'd slide right out of the corners. Things change with time, but I've never seen a track change that fast."

Wood is not complaining, though.

"I'm glad I was brought up at Star," he says. "It taught me how to drive in traffic."

Actually, a racetrack is in a constant state of change.

"When it gets cold," says Dion, "that can really turn a race into single file. Whether early or late in the season, there's only one warm spot on the track. That's the line everyone is using."

Even that line can change with the temperature.

"Generally what happens," says Weeden, "is that when the sun comes out most tracks have a tendency to loosen up."

This tendency creates a repeatable pattern.

"Most of the time if you show up for practice and get the car working right then after dark the car tightens up. Then if it's a long race with the rubber on the track it will loosen up again."

This phenomenon can make a race interesting.

"Let's say it's a track where guys usually race at night and ten-to-15 guys usually race tight," says Weeden. "Then you have a day-race, and some guy wins that hasn't run too good. He may have been running too tight, and now his car works."

That's when you'll hear the guys who normally are fast complaining the loudest.

"There's always a number of people dissatisfied with a track," Dion points out, adding "We've always tried to capitalize on tracks nobody likes. Why complain? We just figure we'd work harder, and those tracks are the places we've done best."

Wood sums up the subject from the perspective he shares with Seymour, Weeden and Dion.

"The bottom line is we're all at the same track, and we all have to drive on it."

Side by side, if we're lucky.

TURN RIGHT TO HAVE FUN

Newburyport Daily News, 2003. In recent years the number of road courses in New England has doubled, including the rejuvenated Thompson Speedway "Motorsports Park." Oh, what fun.

If you like racing you likely like traditional American oval-track racing more than anything.

You like your racetracks right there in front of you as you sit in the grandstands nursing a cold one and some french fries. You like your starts flying, your corners symmetrical, your straightaways equal, your racecars roaring with American power, your fenders and wheels rubbing, and your finishes close and exciting.

You'll tolerate packed parking lots, lines at concession stands, crowds of fans surrounding you, and amenities that generally fall somewhat short of opulent. But hey, racing is a tough business and you're a tough customer. Leave the pastoral settings to those ``wine-and-cheese-set" road racing fans.

It's amazing how turned off by road racing most oval-track-racing fans can be. They complain that road racing is boring or they can't follow a race because they can't see the entire racetrack. They have no interest in little racecars. They only enjoy racing when the cars involved are all over each other, not spread out over a long track. They look at road racers as wusses, idly ambling along in courteous bliss, afraid to scratch their precious racecars.

Most of those impressions is false, based on misinformation, or misses the point entirely.

Standing-starts can be breathtaking when the cars involved are identical, as they often are in the spec classes of road racing. In some spec classes the cars racing are so well-matched that they're wheel to wheel over the course's entire length.

And when that length is filled with every type of corner imaginable, watching the field thrash its way through a race can be a pretty wild experience. Most fans can find themselves one corner or another that produces as much action as an entire short oval might. After all, where a circle tracker soon learns that smooth driving yields the best lap times, road racers learn the exact opposite. Road racers stay on the gas to the last possible instant as they approach a corner, and then they grab every bit of brake they can get their feet on. Nothing courteous about that.

If the only road racing you've seen was in Winston Cup, you've seen nothing of decent road racing. Those big, bulky taxi-cab Cup cars can't get out of their own way, and many Cup drivers can't either. There are some basic techniques in road racing many Cup drivers don't even bother to learn. Lazy slugs.

Nothing lazy about road racers. Or wussy, either. Remember all those rainouts to start the season? In April, while most racers were still huddled in front of their Winston Cup coverage, the Sports Car Club of America was holding races on New Hampshire International Speedway's tricky road course.

``We qualified in the rain,'' one road racer recalled later, ``in cool weather and with a little bit of a snowbank on the outside of the track. But by afternoon the sun came out and the track was pretty dry.''

Keep in mind that these cars run specified tires; there are no slicks for dry conditions. One tire fits all. For the most part the only adjustments allowed here must be made by adjusting, as the saying goes, ``the nut holding the wheel.''

Yet there they were, their track ringed with snow, battling with each other like a bunch of rabid strictly stockers at Hudson Speedway. And there you were, watching another 500 miles of drivers going around in circles on TV.

Okay, I like oval-track racing, too, but don't you owe it to yourself to check out this different form of your favorite sport? Tell you what. Let's start out easy. The Thirteenth Annual Vintage Celebration at NHIS started Wednesday. Tomorrow through Sunday the road course veterans will have their chance to shine on New Hampshire's 1.6-mile road course. Gates open 8 a.m. Admission to the infield and garages is available . You can wander around and see some of the most incredible and exotic vintage sports cars the sport ever produced. Some cars will have values in the five-figure range, yet their drivers will be out there thrashing them like old mini stocks.

And there won't be no lines.

WE'RE NUTS

From Shorttrack Magazine, *2008*

We're all nuts. I mean you, me, everybody who reads this magazine, and everybody who doesn't but shares our love of shorttrack racing. Accept this proposition if you want to understand the depths of our passion.

I started thinking about this after writing that shorttrack racing seemed to be weathering the increasingly putrid economy rather well. That thought still was lurking somewhere in my evidently deranged mind when I heard a report on how fuel prices were impacting summer-vacation plans for many Americans. The report included comments from a woman who was lamenting the fact that her husband and she had been compelled to cancel a European vacation and were instead settling for a stateside beach-rental. She got me wondering why someone who even thought of jetting to Europe (and then had to "settle" for renting a beach-house for a couple of weeks) would be put off by airline tickets going up a few hundred dollars. And then I read that vacation-rentals on Cape Cod were setting records as more and more people decided they, too, would have to settle for a week or two on the Cape. I tried to imagine how much money you might have if renting a house among the priciest summer-properties in New England was your idea of settling. And why, if you could put your hands on that kind of coin, you'd think you had to settle in the first place.

Then I thought about the state of racing in New England. Yes, there are places where car-counts are down, just like there are every year. And just like every year, it's possible that any track that's suffering a loss of cars can point to a non-economic factor at work.

On the other hand, there are healthy turnouts of racecars at many tracks. And since in most of these cases the numbers are up in lower divisions, I'd assumed that this was a racing version of the settling to which many tourists were resorting. But then I realized that this theory didn't really hold water. These new street stock and mini-sprint racers weren't getting out of pro stocks and mods, they were, as always, getting into racing. The guys who were getting out of pro stocks and modifieds must have been hanging up their helmets as well as parking their racecars.

And these weren't cases of common sense. No one was saying to their spouses, "Honey, I probably shouldn't go racing this year. Maybe we can just save some money. Let's rent a house on the Cape."

No. They were losing sponsors. They were losing business. They weren't worrying about spending too much money. They were *out of* money. It wasn't that they saw it would be tougher to race. Tougher they could handle. We're talking impossible.

If you want to analyze the common sense of racers, consider a couple who did step back from a serious competitive racing effort. I figured for sure there'd be condos by now where All-Star Speedway still stands. But, no, racer Bobby MacArthur bought the place and is running an actual racetrack there. Not only that, he jettisoned such (relatively) sensible divisions as roadrunners and V-6 modifieds in favor of bringing back pro stocks, introducing a true modified division and scheduling dates for supers! This is not a business plan any sane consultant would propose.

And when Ralph Nason pulled the plug on the season at Unity, George Fernold stepped up within days to lease the place. He's running a racetrack, too. What could be wiser than that? How about buying stock in Ford Motor Company?

You and I do not escape scorn. I've decided that I simply have to get up to Caribou to Spud Speedway this year. This despite the fact that folks in southern New England believe that Caribou exists only as a post with a thermometer on it. With a lot of numbers below the zero. The gas alone to drive to Caribou will probably set me back more than that woman and her husband would have sprung for their tickets to Europe.

Yeah, I've heard that crowds are down at many tracks. Sure, Mr. Brady rents a movie for his bunch rather than heading out for some fun Saturday evening. But you're still at the track, aren't you? It'll take more than some expensive gas to keep you home. So what if the cupboard is bare? The track's chicken-tenders taste better than ever.

Do they? See, you are nuts.

TIME-TRAVELING
TO NORWAY PINES

From Trackside Magazine, *1998. Today the place is called Legion Speedway. It's still a throwback.*

Drained from a day working amidst exotic British-built racecars and multi-million dollar, chromed, unobtanium racing operations, the race reporters headed north, seeking salvation.

They headed out from the fringes of their modern, digitized, condominiumized society, out into the woods. Soon, as they had been promised, they carne upon a sign that they had found it. A low, block-lettered sign it was; one marking the entrance to a field that provided parking for a few-dozen cars.

The race reporters followed others toward a path disappearing into tall pines. The bluegrass music of Doc Watson – "Tennessee Stud" the song was – wafted from tinny speakers hidden in the trees. Bare bulbs lit the way.

Bent and faded hulks of cars being towed into the woods, not on trailers but by chain, fueled the reporters' curiosity about the track to which they'd journeyed.

After paying a few measly bucks at the combination snack-bar slash ticket booth, they soon found themselves settling into rickety grandstands to watch an evening of racing on the rutted quarter-mile circle of dirt known as Norway Pines Speedway.

They'd driven an hour north from New Hampshire International Speedway – and a quarter-century back in time. They'd found Norway Pines standing, as they'd expected, among its namesake trees. With it, they found one of the last stands of the type of racer that writer Tom Wolfe once referred to as "the Last American Hero." He was the guy (when guys were always "he") with a ton of time and an ounce of cash who cobbled a race car together out of bits of street cars and angle-iron and boiler plate with liberal application of skinned knuckles and colorful words of frustration.

Go to a place like New Hampshire Speedway. Or, these days, even head to what you think of as your local track. After a visit to almost any of these polished places, it will be difficult to avoid the conclusion that backyard artisans are giving way to clean-cut technicians pushing buttons and turning knobs in even more pristine race shops.

But up around Wentworth, NH, racers still were burning insulation out of Chevy Impalas and making their tire selections at the dump. Indeed, it was hard to find a coilover shock, aluminum racing seat or, for that matter, any other aluminum, save for perhaps a few nocturnally-procured state highway street signs, among all of the hardware in the pits that night.

But if this was surprising, the reporters were soon blessed with an even greater shock. The racers at Norway Pines, at least some of them, were actually, saints be praised, racing coupes! The race reporters were thrilled that summer evening to see a half-dozen dirt Modifieds roll toward the green flag clad in bodies stripped from pre-WW II (the big one) Chevies and Fords, harkening back to the heyday of old-timers like Smoky Boutwell and Fred DeSarro.

Before the heats started, the track announcer, sitting in an open booth at eye level with the grandstands, asked the crowd to rise for the national anthem. The reporters peeked in as he cued up an actual record on an ancient hi-fi phonograph player. The player scratched its way through the song, skipping and sliding through "the rockets' red glare" on its quickened way to "the home of the brave." Then the racing began.

The action that unfolded before the reporters that night was crude, rough and honest. Drivers attended to task wearing open-face helmets and grimy T-shirts. One driver, a true throwback in the finest "Bugsy" tradition, clenched a cigar between his gritty teeth.

Racing action was delayed often as the starter climbed down from his flagstand, ambled over to the track's fourth turn, and fired up an ancient water truck or rusting grader to make yet another seemingly futile attempt at grooming the track.

One time the grader quit on the backstretch and the starter patiently strolled over to borrow the battery from another salvaged old truck. Another break in the action came as the track announcer raffled off a ride around the track to a lucky young fan. He took his ride before the racing resumed, sitting on the rear deck of a race car, his legs entering the driver's compartment through the broken-out rear window.

The race reporters soon found themselves wandering over to the garden-shed that served as the track's souvenir booth. One of them purchased a ball cap lettered with the name of the track, although he knew he'd never wear it. It was one of those ugly foam-and-net things popular in the '70s. Someone at the track probably considered them a concession to modem tastes. He bought it anyway. However quaint or ugly it might have been, it still was one piece of the place – and the time it represented – that he could take away with him.

And then the racing resumed. The mods also included rough copies of DIRT-style cars with bodies fashioned from sheet metal mMods ran with six-cylinder power. One half-expected to find inline motors plucked from '53 GMC pick-ups under the crude tin hoods of the fastest cars. Innovation was everywhere and, in true shadetree fashion, much of it made little sense to the educated eye. Wings, for instance, sprouted at ungodly angles from the roofs of a few cars. Some wings sported odd side panels that could serve no earthly purpose.

Other divisions raced that night as well. Crumpled jalopies competed as "Late Model Dirt Stockers." Four-cylinder Toyotas and Pintos buzzed around the track. Fans followed the action with enthusiasm. Entire families wolfed down burgers and inhaled Cokes. Nubile young girls showed off their latest already-out-of-fashion fashions on the arms of chain-smoking boys dressed in greasy gas station finery. Middle-aged men, dressed as if they'd just stepped from an episode of "The Fall Guy" talked among themselves knowingly. And the race-reporters sat among them, enjoying the show in appropriate slack-jawed awe. They knew

66

they'd be back any time a Saturday evening found them anywhere near State Route 25 in Wentworth.

They knew one other thing as well. They knew that tomorrow, after they made their way past the hospitality-tents and through the obnoxious television crews, they would watch the exotic, computer-designed, British-built racecars about which they were assigned to report from a new and much healthier perspective.

THE RACEDAY EXPERIENCE

From Trackside Magazine, *2002. Of course, there is no more Whip City Speedway. Rental rides, however, still exist.*

Racers have a hard relationship with time. It is not their friend. That's obvious enough to anyone standing thumb-to-stopwatch, measuring the qualifying times of drivers out on the track. When a half-second can separate the entire field for some races, the tiniest measurable fractions of time have the power to make or ruin a weekend, a series, or even a career.

But the race against time is continual, year-round and ongoing in every phase of preparation. It's why every move a driver makes off the track as well as on it is made with the ever-present factor of time looming over it.

This is a point you can learn just racing as a hobbyist. Reporters do well to keep it in mind whenever they visit a racetrack on raceday. Wise ones keep discussions with racers to a minimum, contacting them during the week to get the meat of stories and then touching base with drivers only briefly as they prepare for competition. Still, the point can be lost to the pressure of publication deadlines, those measurements of time that loom over their own work.

But if these lessons might have gotten obscured in recent years they were reinforced in June when I drove a mini-sprint owned by Ed and Paul Baillargeon in competition at Whip City Speedway. My assignment was to experience what drivers go through at a race and then describe it for *Trackside* readers There was much to learn about preparing, driving and racing these potent little cars on the broad dirt oval that lies under the approach-pattern of the airport in Westfield, MA. But it was the significance of time to a racer that was the message I came away from my adventure wanting to share. The thrill I'd experience, well, that would be harder to share. Besides, who would want to?

The idea for this story, not surprisingly, was my own. Let's be honest. The biggest perk of this beat is the chance to drive what I watch others race. I've been given more than one opportunity to do that, and I've never said no. But those opportunities have always come on a weekday at an otherwise closed racetrack with the entire track to myself and all the time in the world. Admittedly you don't climb into a supermodified without some apprehension, even if you've got the whole track to yourself and a corps of people focused on avoiding damage to their machine and, incidently, embarrassment to you. But it is not racing.

I wanted to share the pressures racers face as they get ready to put everything on the line in a situation where their participation means nothing to anyone outside their team and attention must be seized from a group of competitors equally determined to themselves be the center of attention. I wanted to take readers into the pits, into the trailer, and ultimately into the racecar as a race team prepared to go into battle.

The fact that I'd be the one driving would be the gravy. Credit and thanks belong to my bosses here at *Trackside*, publishers Steve Pighetti and Cindi Hopkins, for providing the opportunity. They'd been part of the racing scene at Whip City for years. That's the sort of inside line you need if you're going to convince some driver to step out of his car and let someone else, and a writer, no less, go racing in it.

That's exactly what they convinced Carl Sherman to do. Sherman agreed not only to let me drive his ride but to relinquish his practice time as well as his place in the evening's heat race to me. The fact that the Baillargeons would let any stranger into one of their cars to do anything based simply on their faith in and friendship with Steve and Cindi – well, this was more than I had any right to expect.

But that was the plan as it came together just days before my race-date. Which, of course, immediately put time at a premium. Yet when I contacted Sherman by phone he wasn't concerned about time, even when I referred to it specifically with simple questions about when I needed to arrive.

``You don't need to get there too early. I usually try to get there by four. There's a lot of waiting around, a lot of time to kill. It's best not to get there too early."

But I had my concerns. I decided to arrive at least a half-hour before that and in fact had signed in at the pit gate by about 3:15. And found that I'd beaten my racecar to the track. So I headed to the pit grandstands and watched some of the action as the karts raced through the afternoon on Whip City's inner oval.

Saturday afternoons at Whip City belong to the karts. A bunch of different divisions for kids and adults race on what appears to be about an eighth-mile oval inside the quarter-mile circuit I'd roll onto as evening settled in. Each week one of the kart divisions also is part of the track's evening race card.

Meanwhile the red box trailer I'd been on the lookout for had rolled in behind me. By the time I noticed and got over to their pit spot the team already had rolled out its two cars and was getting ready to prep them for the evening's racing.

Care to look closely enough and you'll find that mini-sprints are impressive machines despite their small stature. For one thing they're thoroughbred racecars, not cobbled together out of spare parts but crafted out of competition-components. There are no remnants of burned-out insulation to be found in one. Getting into a mini-sprint is like putting on a tuxedo compared to climbing into the coveralls environment of a typical street stock.

And dismissing the motorcycle-derived engines found in these cars would be a mistake. Most cars in the 600cc class with which I'd be racing, including my ride, utilize engines from Honda's CBR600 street bikes. Honda's engineers are among the best in the world and they are after serious power when they design CBR-series motorcycles. A year ago on a visit to Whip City I'd talked to Steve Robinson, a former president of the Granite State Mini Sprint Association who ran a 600 Honda. He'd found that there was little point to looking for more power from the motor than Honda already had provided.

Before this season, however, Whip City decided to allow teams to swap the vacuum-diaphragm carbs that come from Honda with flat-slide carbs. The thinking was that throttle response would be quickened noticeably with the carb slides mechanically connected to the throttle by cable rather than being opened via motor-induced vacuum. While Robinson and many other teams stuck with the stock carbs, the Baillargeons made the switch.

``The thinking was that you'd get the quicker throttle-response and it'd also be easier to run the car with less loading up and some other problems the stock carbs have," related Sherman. ``We've been having problems with (making them work) all season, though."

The problems had so far contributed to a tough season, off Sherman's regular pace as one of the division's most successful drivers. But this is not a team that rests on its laurels. The challenge posed by the new carbs on Sherman's car were nothing compared to that of running Yamaha's R6 engine in the car driven by Ed Baillargeon, Jr. Fans of Superbike road racing will tell you this is the hot 600cc engine to have. But committing to racing a

Yamaha-powered mini-sprint is akin to running Mopar or Ford power with the World of Outlaws, or anywhere else, for that matter.

``We're getting there with it," reported Ed, Jr., who nonetheless seemed to enjoy its potential ``It's fast."

I talked a little with Sherman as Ed Sr., and crew members Luke Ogonowski and Dan Ashe poured over the two cars. I'd driven a couple of times on dirt back before Sugar Hill Speedway was paved (Wow! Just like the old-timers from Stafford) but that had been years ago. What, I wanted to know, was the process of turning a fast lap on the wide Whip City oval, with its moderate banking, apparently smooth, dry surface and short straights? Sherman started to describe the process by repeating what he'd told me in our phone conversation.

``The faster you go the easier it is to drive," he again declared. ``Actually, it's a pretty easy track to run. The straights are pretty short and you've got plenty of room. You can carry your speed right up almost to the fence on the front straight. Just leave a little bit of room in case you get bumped on the inside. On the back straight you'll never get near the wall."

I asked about braking. In addition to a turn of the wheel upon entry into a corner, the brakes were one of the tools available to set the car for its slide through the turns. On dirt, of course, you need that slide to carry enough speed through the corners. I knew that the precision of asphalt racing I was used to would be of limited benefit on a racetrack that changed below you and offered limited traction on its best days compared to pavement.

``You really don't need to use the brakes," Sherman explained. ``Maybe just a little tap as you enter the corner. But usually you just can just get off the throttle a second when you turn and it will settle right in."

Amidst introductions to various Whip City regulars and Sherman's discussions with people curious about his evening's plans, time to head to the evening's drivers' meeting arrived. We headed over and joined the circle of drivers gathered around Whip City's head tech man Dave Pighetti. Yes, he's Steve's father.

Whip City's drivers are fortunate when it comes to drivers' meetings. Pighetti was to the point, reinforcing the track's rules about driving through the pits in no uncertain terms due to problems observed in recent weeks.

Drivers' meetings are essential for reminding juiced-up competitors of rules, regulations and expectations that often get lost in the fire of competition. Sometimes, though, they can drag on through discussions over extraneous issues not having an impact on the upcoming racing. Worse, they become beef sessions among disgruntled drivers or soapbox opportunities for officials full of themselves. This meeting was over in minutes, but not before the point that needed to be made got conveyed in no uncertain terms.

But now the evening's practice time loomed before me. We hurried back so I could get fitted into the car. It took three of us – Sherman and Ogonowski providing me with assistance – to get the job done, mostly due to my limited understanding of how the array of belts, restraints and buckles came together. The job hardly was done before the time came to do it for real. I reattached myself to the car right at the trailer and Sherman and Steve Pighetti pushed me to the track entrance. Then Sherman reviewed the starting procedure we'd discussed earlier.

Similar to most racecars, a toggle engaged the ignition. Similar to no sprint cars, a push button turned the engine over, thanks to Honda's electric starting motor. Another toggle switched on the car's electric fuel pump, yet another the car's cooling fan.

``I usually try to shut off the fuel pump during cautions or when I drive through the pits," Sherman explained. ``And I try to turn the fan on in the pits. You probably don't have to worry about that. If you think of it, that's great."

The clutch for the car was disengaged by the bike-style hand lever attached to an arm that manipulated a linkage connected to the shift-shaft, which protruded from the left side of the engine.

``We're going to push you right out onto the track," Steve explained. ``When we get you out there, all the way, you can put it into second and go."

Sherman reached in and fired the car up. Then I shifted into first, promptly killing the engine. I'd forgotten to pull in the clutch lever, stepping on the brake pedal instinctively. Further instruction and another attempt and I felt myself getting pushed onto the track with the engine running. I pulled the shifter back, released the lever and gave it the gas. The car lurched forward as I maintained a slow pace.

The car felt rough and struggled against me to turn into the track's infield. At this speed its natural inclination to turn left was a nuisance.

As I passed under the starter's stand I saw the starter rotating the furled yellow flag in the air. I picked up speed slightly and then noticed everyone else barging by. I'd expected to see an unfurled green to signal the start of hot laps but it immediately was obvious that we were at speed.

I gave it more gas as I entered turn-one and kept feeding the engine as I exited two. Then I booted it and felt the rush of acceleration. That is the drug to which every racer is addicted.. I've felt it in some of the fastest cars to race on shorttracks. The mini sprint gave me enough of a fix to satisfy my racing jones.

Entering three I dabbed at the brakes, turned left and, even at my slow pace, felt the car's rear end slide out tentatively. It was easy to continue to feed it more power. Out of four I gassed it again and for the first time felt myself with some real speed to scrub off. Again a bit of brake and a nudge of the wheel and I could feel the effect on the car's direction.

In the few laps available for practice I concentrated on two things, getting into the power as soon as my nerve would allow through the corners and out of them, and hanging on as long as my nerve would allow approaching them. Each time I got passed I'd

74

try to pick my pace up to that of the passing car, and I found I could match their pace at least for a few moments. What I wasn't doing was putting together any sort of smooth lap or getting a real sense of a racing line all the way around.

Man, though, Sherman was absolutely right. The faster I went the smoother the car felt and the more it began to help me out, as if it understood my goals and shared them with me. Part of that, it goes without saying, was because I wasn't close to finding the car's own limits.

Practice seemed over in seconds. As I made my way off the track I remembered the switches for the fan and fuel pump and tried to find them. Now, my Simpson helmet is an uncompromising piece of protection and I love that fact, but it wasn't designed for looking at your feet. There was no way I could find the switches without turning down to locate them visually. I did find them, but a pylon was victimized in the process.

Still, folks offered praise for my efforts.

``I'm impressed," admitted Sherman, for one. ``You did way better than I thought you would."

Steve Robinson offered his point of view as gained out on the track.

``I followed you a while. You had a pretty good line. You were going good."

Big mistake, of course. Now I felt eager to get back out there and mix it up with the competition. First I'd have to catch them. As a rookie in his first race I'd start from the back row, bright yellow rookie tape streaming behind me with no one to heed its warning – for the entire race, I hoped.

For once, I was not surprised by the arrival of the next event of the agenda, my heat race. Both Baillargeon and Robinson were slated to race in the first 600 heat with me in the second. As soon as Baillargeon headed out I readied myself with the help of Ogonowski. This time I fired the car up at the trailer and drove it to the track. Then I waited.

Any race driver will tell you. A racecar at rest is the most uncomfortable environment in the world. Part of the reason is the car itself, and some cars are worse than others. Racecars are built to be fast and sometimes the driver appears to be almost an afterthought. Take a close look at the cockpit of a midget some time. The mini sprint was not as bad as that, but the bulging engine on the car's left side took up a lot of leg room.

Worse than ergonomics is the simple fact that you get in one to go fast. If a car gets better as it goes faster how bad must it be at a standstill? Most drivers work out to the second how soon they want to be in the car and ready to go. Too soon and they get restless, uncomfortable, or worse. Too late and they're compelled to rush, hastily buckling up and never having a moment to make sure they and their cars are ready.

Later in the evening, while Sherman waited for 600 feature to roll off the grid, Paul Baillargeon would discuss with me the difficulty of being forced to wait for the 250cc micro sprints, which typically raced before the 600 division.

``They don't go three laps without a yellow. It's tough to be sitting in your car, buckled up with your helmet on, while they take all that time to finish."

For my heat race time to go came soon enough. Again Sherman and Steve Pighetti pushed me out. I hurried to catch up to the field of six cars and find my slot on the inside of the third row. It was time for the green.

I'd already decided that I would key my start off of that of the driver in front of me. I'd been involved in enough rolling starts to get it, and I knew that it wasn't unusual to run right up into a less than alert driver lined up in front of you.

These guys were plenty alert. By the time I gassed it the cars in front of me were gone. By the time I was into turn-one the pack was on the back straight. That was a margin that remained constant, though. And more than that, the car that lined up to my outside was not among them. He still was behind me.

With all this open track I focused on smooth and consistent laps. I again wanted to improve with each corner. I did that. But my growing success, combined with the words of encouragement I'd received from Sherman and others earlier, had left me with perhaps a little too much confidence. I knew I'd been pinching down coming onto each straight, keeping lower than the line. This was scrubbing off speed. As I approached the white-flag lap I made a conscious decision to get on the gas and let the car carry its speed up to the outside of the front straight.

It sure did that. It shot up toward the fence before I knew it. I tried to get off the throttle while I steered it to the left. Just as I did I felt the right-rear slap the rail, forcing the car straight again. You can insert your favorite expletive here. It won't be far from what I hollered as I turned it away from the fence and got on it again.

Surprisingly, though, I still didn't see the red number-25 that had started outside me. I brought the car home a lap later right where I started, fifth out of six cars. As far as I was concerned there was victory enough in that.

My night was over. For the serious guys the heat represented only the opening act of their performances. For Sherman it represented the start of his night, two track sessions and several laps after everyone else had begun racing. Handicapped by starting last on the field Sherman began his charge immediately, instantly demonstrating how well the car handled on the outside of the track. Unfortunately the field split into two fast groups. Sherman never made it out of the second one before he got together with another car and spun in turn-four. Lining up scratch on the field again for the restart he never had a chance to compete for a top spot.

I had accomplished everything I'd hoped for. I'd experienced the emotions felt by racers every time they sign the entry form. The growing concentration as the time to race approached, the intense focus as preparation got underway, the heavy heartbeats while buckled in ready to go out, the absolute, sheer joy of stepping on the gas and feeling the charge down the track, the exhilaration of sliding through a corner, the satisfaction of meeting the challenge, the pleasure of reliving it afterwards with those who were a part of the experience, all those feelings came to me, even though my effort was as a guest, a visitor to a world in which these racers are immersed.

But there's no reason we have to envy racers. Whip City proves every Saturday that thrills don't have to come from bigtime racing to be bigtime. Plenty of people experience them even from racing karts - or slot cars, for that matter.

It's like the old saying about the dog in the fight. It's not the car in the race that makes it thrilling, it's the race in the car. Don't take my word for it. Get yourself out there. You can rent a dwarf car or a 250 mini-sprint to race at Whip City. You can buy a kart cheap. Rental time in racing karts is a growing trend. Or go do one of those driving experiences.

You know you love racing. Go find out why.

LOCAVORE RACING

From Shortrrack Magazine, *2008. I've been a locavore for a long time, for entertainment as well as dinner.*

Oh, and I have no idea what was in Michael's carb.

If the experts are to be believed, the world is moving unceasingly toward a global economy. With every merger, every acquisition. every new mega-company created by hostile takeover, we find ourselves closer to a world made flat by technology and ever-increasing and concentrated wealth.

We see this phenomenon hit home when a new WalMart undercuts the business not only of mom-and-pop operations but even department stores that once were regional institutions. We see it when our local blues or classical-music radio station becomes a hip-hop or "The Hits ofthe 70s and 80s!" outlet after quietly becoming the six-millionth acquisition by Clear Channel.

We see it in racing, too. CASCAR always was a neat little late-model series racing north ofthe border. Now it's NASCAR Way-North, pushing upon contrary Canadians their own flavor of NASCAR. We are excited here to see USAC's Silver Crown Series come to New Hampshire International in September, but many claim that it wouldn't have happened without NASCAR. Some contend that NASCAR's ultimate goal is to purchase USAC outright in order to expand its sanctions to more tracks than can accommodate its headlining NEXTEL Cup Series.

Pessimistic economists swear that someday we'll see one corporation grow larger than any other, larger even than any country, in control of the entire world. Whether that corporation winds up being NASCAR or Toyota depends largely upon what substance was in Michael's carburetor.

This sort of paranoia has led to much gnashing of teeth. Those who protest that NASCAR is killing local racing believe there is no way the local bullring can present a show as exciting as a big-league racing telecast with its steamroller of America's star-making machinery. This is the same train of thought that leads some to question how the local hardware store can sell a rake as cheaply as Home Depot when the local store purchases 15 rakes to Home Depot's 15,000.

I'd never apply that reasoning to racing, as regular readers of my ravings already know. The news here, however, is that some economists are becoming skeptical as well.

According to a recent piece in the *Boston Globe*, "The momentum in the economy has begun a small, still barely-discernable shift toward the local and away from the global."

The Globe offers examples of this trend. Are you aware, for instance, that in the midst of WalMart's forays into the grocery business and the expansion of Stop & Shops to the point they are installing rest-areas every 15 aisles, the greatest expansion in the grocery business is in farmers' markets? The Globe even reports that in western Mass., the locals launched their own currency, which can be obtained at area banks and soon even ATMs.

Other reports site a longing on the part of some consumers for real customer-service. Being in the habit of ignoring ignorant Home Depot employees who know less about their own store or construction than I do, I can vouch for the appeal of the local hardware store. When its warped wooden floor starts squeaking under my feet, I know the grumpy clerk will know exactly what I'm looking for, where to find it and how to install it.

I also know that I can turn on a NEXTEL Cup race on TV and nothing will seem any different from when I turned it on an hour – or week – ago. Now, that includes the cars themselves, never mind the drivers. Find two drivers in Cup today as different from each other as Cale and Richard. Fat chance. Neither of them would get a ride.

Bigtime TV racing has created hordes of new fans who realize auto racing is a pretty cool sport. Imagine if some of them realize that minutes from home they can find fire-fighters racing factory-workers racing politicians, in cars as slick as the ones on TV plus some a galaxy slicker than anything in StarWars and some more ragged than garbage trucks. Imagine what they'd think if they felt – felt! – a field of supers roar by their faces. Imagine after their jaws dropped at the sight of midgets or modifieds racing nose to tail if they realized 20 minutes later they were standing next to the kid who won the race. Imagine what their own kids would think.

Now, get out there and tell them what they're missing when they miss local racing.

IN
MY
OPINION

THE SHORTTRACK MANIFESTO

From Shorttrack Magazine, 2004. *This remains my personal manifesto when it comes to racing.*

There's an old saying, `If you don't stand for something you'll probably stand for anything."

Well, if you publish a magazine it should probably stand for something. This is the time to declare what it is *Shorttrack* stands for. Consider it, if you will, the *Shorttrack* Manifesto. It starts with a declaration that would seem self-evident; that not all racing is created equal.

Shorttrack racing is the sport's greatest form. For racers it tends to equalize equipment and minimize the influence of complicating forces such as pit crews, fuel management, expensive technology, and all that other stuff we hear discussed too much in regard to other forms of racing (Oh my goodness! Michael Shumacher lost!). It also creates a means to reduce expenses.

For the fans it's even better. Sit down. Watch the race. See every inch and every second of it. Get up. Get a hotdog. Sit down. See every inch and every second of the next race.

For both, it maximizes the possibility that the racing will be close, down to the wire, can't stay in your seat, exciting. Three times over the course of the evening.

Every shorttrack is a wonderful place. See Stafford. First-class all the way. Great drivers. A big, tough track with a heritage of awesome proportions. A show filled with action presented by a trained and dedicated group of professionals. The place is clean, safe; a great place to bring the family.

Go to Star. If the town has let it open. The place is ragged, unkempt. "Watch for splinters in the stands!" The restrooms are, are, well, try to hold it. The track is wide, then it's narrow. There's that wall. Then there's woods. Cars have been lost out there for months. Every race features drivers trying to disprove that basic law of physics, "No two things can occupy one place at the same time." At any one time there is a group of drivers who are vowing they will never return to the place. They always do. So do I. I love the place as much as I do Stafford.

Shorttrack people invariably are great people. Actually, racing people are great people. Don't take this for granted. I've covered stick-and-ball sports a little. Pro sports revolve around a system perfectly designed to create self-centered, insincere spoiled-rotten jerks. They start them young, too.

Racers are self-made. The best of them did it on their own, or with little help beyond mom and dad. They know they're lucky. Drivers mean it when they say they're having fun. If fists or words fly it's usually over the racing, not over a contract or because people think it sells tickets (even though it does).

I worry a little about all the young kids who are on the path to racing stardom before they've outgrown their jammies. It seems to me to be too much like what basketball does to kids. Still, every time I've dealt with one of the kids I worry about I find I like and respect them as much as the older guys I like and respect. Maybe the moms and dads are just better people than the hockey parents I see screaming at each other at some pee wee game.

This is racing's heritage. I'm a sucker for those free magazine deals, you know, where they offer you an issue free and then sign you up unless you mark the bill "cancel" (Forget it. We can't afford it). I received this new mag that professed to be about racing, and hunting and fishing and girls and trucks. Nice combination. Actually it professed to be about Nextel Cup racing.

In the editor's column he talked about why Cup racing had grown so big in the last five or so years. One of his big reasons was that in the last few years racetracks had sprung up all over the country, not just in the South!

Just thought you'd want to know. You never saw Mario drive a Midget at Thompson, or Richard drive a Grand National car there ("What's Grand National?"). Never mind Richie, or Fred, or Bugsy. Mods can't claim to be the oldest division in NASCAR. They didn't exist.

We're perfectly comfortable here at *Shorttrack*, right where we are, covering this, the best form of the sport, in the best place to see it. We'll leave the rest to such fools as him.

SPORTING GOODS

From Trackside Magazine, *1998. In a way the inspiration for this column no longer even exists. I can't tell you the last time I saw a racing column in a daily newspaper. I haven't contributed one in almost a decade.*

Anybody who covers racing for a daily newspaper is bound to get defensive after awhile. In a neighborhood as crowded as a typical daily's sports page, writers are fighting for every inch they can get, and if there's any sense that an interloper is in their midst, sportswriters are quick to protest.

Many of them are notorious, anyway, for forming opinions without stooping to the laborious chore of gathering facts. These cretins have been conditioned to the idea that because their ugly mugs adorn their copy, their views, no matter how mis-or-uninformed, will be consumed without question by get-a-lifers even less concerned with reality than they are.

My first gig writing about racing in a daily is my favorite example. It came as the.result of a panicked response to an avalanche of mail received by a Massachusetts paper after its sports editor wrote that race fans would enjoy their "sport" (his quotes, not mine) even more if good ole' boys were strapped to the hood of each car. This ignorant slop resulted in the most overwhelming response to any story ever published in the paper, and I'm forever grateful for the opportunity all you folks who wrote created for me.

But I still have to lobby for racing at that paper. The latest sports editor there will do stuff like bury a paragraph on Loudon's Winston Cup race under a sports-short about a European golf tournament, ignoring the more than 90,000 fans who attended the race with a claim that there just isn't that much interest in racing. D'uh.

So excuse me if I remain a bit defensive, but it still bothers me when I visit the paper and a couple of its more grizzled sportswriters take shots at me, making vroom-vroom noises or cracks about yokels. One guy, who figures he's in the know because he got drunk in the infield at Daytona while in college, uses all sorts of specious logic to argue against the acceptance of racing as a legitimate sport. And one of his favorite lines of logic has to do with a racer's reliance on technology as the means to victory. That got me steaming a little recently as I read a sports article in a magazine to which I subscribe.

The magazine is "Goalies World," and the story was a critique of Ron Tugnutt, who tends goal for the National Hockey League's Ottawa Senators. The story made a point about how Tugnutt's game had immediately improved when he made the adjustment of adapting to larger leg pads. What got me was that I gradually realized I was reading what essentially represented "TechKnowledge" for goaltenders.

As one of those happy fools who devotes a number of winter hours to putting my body in front of flying rubber, I spent an inordinate amount of time and energy focused upon my equipment. I'd stitched together two goalies' catching mitts to get one with which I was comfortable, designed and had heli-arced a new wire cage for my helmet, and paid some serious bucks to have a stick-side blocking glove fabricated that utilized an idea I'd seen in a product catalog. Currently I'm sitting on info from a company that will custom-make sticks for me once I send them more money than I should spend for such a foolish thing.

Now, the idea my blocker took advantage of came from the fact that part of its blocking surface overlaps an area already covered by my stick. The sport's rules specify a maximum dimension for this blocking surface but it's more vague concerning the surface's shape. So this pad essentially juts out at an angle along its bottom third or so, covering an area otherwise left open. In theory, even if I didn't move, this pad now could stop a shot that otherwise would be a goal.

That's the same theory exploited a couple of years ago by Garth Snow when he was with the Philadelphia Flyers. He started to wear shoulder pads that seemingly extended past his ears until the NHL came out with new specifications that brought the pads back closer to earth. At the same time, they cracked down on leg pads and other pieces of equipment that had begun to skirt those aforementioned dimension rules. Evidently, then, this makes Garth Snow and me the norm for goaltenders and not a couple of technogeeks who take their cues from, say, racing.

And the analogy flies further than just the idea that some goalies pay close attention to their equipment. As racing has moved away from its "run what ya brung" mentality over the years, so too have many sports moved away from "wear what we sell."

"The stuff that's out there has made huge strides in the last 15 years," agreed Joe Bertagna in a recent conversation. Bertagna should know. He played goalie for years – decades, in fact. His best years as a player came at Harvard University, where he often made do by adapting equipment from other sports or just settling for inferior performance. Guys who raced stock cars in the '60s can relate.

Bertagna later spent some time as goalie coach for the Boston Bruins and currently runs the Joe Bertagna Goalie School, one of the most successful goalie schools in North America. He also serves on the rules-making committee for the National Collegiate Athletic Association. So he keeps current on the state of the game and its related technology. From this perspective he makes another observation that will sound familiar to those who have followed racing for a long time.

"Almost all the fear has been taken out of playing goal," he stated. "It affects the way you approach an opponent, and how you play the game."

This, then, has just reinforced the importance of technical skills over the sheer bravery of, say, Terry Sawchuk, who hung his face out to become perhaps the greatest goalie in the history of the game, much the way A.J. Foyt did on his own path to greatness.

Of course Foyt's preference for building his own cars is a thing of the past, as well. But the technologists' impact on racing is duplicated in the

90

craft of designing and fabricating goalie equipment.

"(Manufacturers) are designing pads for the way a guy plays," Bertagna maintained. "You get some goalies who handle the puck a lot so they won't want a deep glove. The catching glove you put on may feel horrible but it's perfect for someone else."

That custom fit has become a crucial element of success in almost every sport. Ed Kirby has seen the same trend in golf in his years as a PGA touring pro and while running Kirby's Golfhouse, a Rhode Island pro shop and school.

"We do custom clubs here," he explained recently. "Very seldom do we give someone a club off the rack. The clubs have to fit you. People are more and more into equipment than ever before. There's a lot to this business; grip-size, shaft-size."

It's more than just fit, though. After all, even your shoes have to fit. But in golf, Kirby can identify key technological advances that have had immediate impact on the game.

"Titanium made a big difference with the wood market," he said. "Oversize heads made a big difference in the driver market. Players will definitely notice with the oversize heads that their contact is better. Then their confidence will definitely rise and they'll drive longer, too."

In describing these new innovations Kirby reveals another similarity to stick-and-ball sports. "I think the long putter is something veterans are not real pleased with," he admitted. "I think the (Professional Golfers Association) and the USGA will begin to limit how long clubs can be. People are saying, 'Wait a minute. The club and the ball should be the same."

So is equipment any more important in racing than it is in other sports? Well, Ed Kirby made a point about his customers and then went on to relate it to his own view of racing. We'll let him have the final word.

"The better you are the more important equipment is," he related. "However, the better the player the more they can do with anything.

"It's like a race driver. Nobody can win if the car is no good. On the other hand you can't buy a game."

BASSCAR?

For a short time in 2017 I contributed a column to the website, RaceChasers Online. *Then I submitted this one and never heard from them again. Was it something I said?*

We all have our favorite afflictions. We all have our tics, our habits, our obnoxious obsessions. We also have our hobbies, our pastimes, and our – well – obnoxious obsessions. Sometimes our hobbies are afflicted by our obsessions, and sometimes our hobbies *are* our obsessions. I think that's the difference between being a baseball fan and being a Boston Red Sox fan.

In racing, folks who wear a jacket that mimics the sponsor-saturated driving suit of their favorite racer are letting their obsessions get in the way of their hobby. So is the guy who hates some driver he doesn't even know. Either way, with love or hatred, they insist on taking too seriously what is after all, supposed to be about entertainment.

Then there are the folks who insist on constantly reinventing the wheels that drive their favorite racing. They're the ones who whine about the need to lower expenses in some division and then whine even more when a crate motor is approved, or complain about wings on sprinters, or spec tires (or *no* spec tires) for late models, or the fact that streeters somewhere can run fabricated bodies that don't even match what's under them. Or, taking it a step further, complain simply that stock cars aren't stock anymore.

You know. Guys like me.

If you've been reading my column here, you read recently where I speculated about the viability of a division of cars created from the same recipe that spawned the first racers called "modifieds." I wondered then if a track could host a division and say essentially "anything goes," as long as that anything came out of some vehicle manufactured for the street.

My mind raced with thoughts of builders cobbling together cars built on pickup-truck rails with pickup-truck rears and bodies peeled from two-door Civics and Corollas – or maybe a body from some old rotted-out Vega or Pinto.

You might recall I contacted Art Barry and Dave Berghman, two guys who have been around mods since they first sported that Vega and Pinto sheet-metal. They were not even interested enough in the idea to be unimpressed by it.

That never stops me. I continue to wonder, "What will be the future of the racing we call "stock car?" Will short-track racing become saturated with Civics and Corollas – entire Civics and Corollas – the likes of such cars becoming the main ingredient in the streeters of the future? Is the rear-wheel drive racecar simply obsolete? What backyard low-buck creation will be the first step to stardom for the future aspirants to NASCAR, IndyCar or F-1?"

Will the pieces be there to build what you can't afford to buy? Could someone create an extremely inexpensive chassis that would accept Honda or, say, Ford Focus power and maybe utilize suspension, wheels and other pieces from a donor car otherwise relegated to the crusher line? Maybe a little late-model lite with minimal need for high-buck parts?

See how easy it is for me to drift off into happy daydreams about cars that don't exist? Like more inexpensive entry-level open wheelers. Think of those mini-supers that utilize a high-revving motorcycle motor to make their motive power, but rear-engined; a Formula for low-cost racing.

I could go on. A track building a fleet of identical street stocks and then renting them out on a race-by-race basis as a one-design series for would-be and casual racers. A division for old Cup cars that specifies crate motors and spec shocks and tires – tires with the stickiness of sewer-covers.

Did I tell you about my idea for a short-track event on the NASCAR Cup calendar with heats, a consi and a 50-lap feature? Maybe at Bristol? C'mon. You can't tell me you don't like *that* idea.

I recall one time when this process got particularly interesting. I was at NHIS (Yes, "I" then, not "M") sharing a camper with my photographer-brother John and columnist- brother Paul and passing time by talking about nothing important. We got to thinking about divisions we'd like to see. I'm sure I started the conversation.

This was just after NASCAR had introduced its truck division. It was late, and we were bored. If pickups were acceptable racecars, then we figured just about anything could be.

"How 'bout panel trucks," I suggested. "Wouldn't you pay to see a Snap-On truck out there trading paint with a UPS van or Safe-T- Clean truck?"

Face it. There would be a lot of paint there to trade.

As for pickups, I suggested that having pickup trucks race was pointless – unless they carried something.

"How about toolboxes?" said I. "Or whatever it is their sponsor sells?"

But it was John who had the best idea.

"They should make them tow boats."

Wouldn't that be great? You could wreck the car you're trying to pass, or just wreck the boat.

John even had a name for his new series.

"They could call it 'BASSCAR.'"

I'd pay to see that, too.

So. You got any suggestions?

SMARTS

From Shorttrack Magazine, *2005. Nothing's changed.*

Those who know me, and even those who've just read my stuff for a while, might be aware that I worked in the human-service field for some time; still have my hands in it, actually, as this baby you hold in your hands grows from infancy.

Specifically, my specialty always involved helping survivors of strokes and head injuries return to work. This occupation provided special perspective as I watched the racing industry deal with the issues of brain-injury in the sport. That's a whole other subject for another day (or; "Don't get me started...").

Needless to say, I've learned a lot about the brain, how it functions – and how it malfunctions. I've also learned about the nature of intelligence in general. I've worked with some real experts, professionals in medicine and psychology who have spent their lives studying the gray matter between our ears and what is going on in that lump of soggy fat.

I got to thinking about this recently while on another adventure with my good friend Greg St. Hilaire. Greg's been around racing longer than he'd care for me to share with you, although I've only known him a couple of years. He's made a habit of inviting me on excursions where we drop in, often unannounced, upon unsuspecting friends of his. This day he'd arranged the visit with Mike Ordway that resulted in our cover story for this issue. But we had some time to kill, so he figured I should meet Bud and Ken Merrick, as they'd watched Mike grow up and into racing. I had a great time listening as these guys reminisced before Bud finally returned to rebuilding the transmission that was supposed to be done that day.

Our next stop was Watts Racing Enterprises. There, he introduced me to Robert and Scott Watts, both of whom I'd spoken to over the years but never actually met face-to-face. Scott in turn gladly introduced us to the dyno at Watts and the amazing software that has turned the black art of building horsepower into an increasingly sophisticated science.

As with everyone to whom Greg has introduced me, the Merricks and the Watts were unfailingly accommodating. Still, I always have the feeling that folks are thinking to themselves, "Wait until I see Greg again. I'll have to straighten him out about this dropping reporters into our laps in the middle of a workday."

This of course is not what I was thinking about as I considered those experts who study the brain. Their relation to racing is mostly non-existent. These academically trained professionals would hardly grant a racer a status above one of their test rats, their prejudice reinforced by waves of rebels flags and piles of crushed Budweiser cans, as seen on TV.

I, however, know the truth. I've heard them speak of how there are different types of intelligence, how different parts of the brain serve different functions, and how strengths in one area quite often can predict a weakness in another specific area.

I've also seen the respected neurologist walk into a building to retrieve his forgotten keys, carry on a ten-second conversation with the receptionist, and leave without the keys. I've been witness to physiatrists as they passionately debated whether their title should be pronounced "fizz- EYE- a-trist" or "FIZZY-a-trist." I've seen a conceited and belligerent physiatrist get insulted because I pronounced it "incorrectly," (Of course I did. It was deliberate.).

I've also watched the mechanic with a sixth-grade education figure out how to disassemble some outrageously complex piece of equipment for the first time and piece it back together weeks later without error. I've watched guys attack some less-then-perfect part of their racecar just for the fun of it and wind up with more power, better grip, quicker turn-in or less weight.

I've seen a technician more comfortable with a wrench in his hand reluctantly tackle a computer program, learn how to use it without a book or use of the "help" menu, and figure out how the masters-level programmer screwed it up.

In short, I've seen a lot of really smart people at work. Some of them wear white lab coats. Some of them, like the guys I was visiting, wear dark-blue shop uniforms, or blue-jeans. Which ones would I rather drop in on? Well, put it this way. If you know Greg, consider yourself warned.

DOPES

From Shorttrack Magazine, *2008.*

It's been fun watching the New England Patriots rampage through the football season, but I have to admit, it's making me a little uncomfortable.

Sure, the team's unprecedented success has been refreshing for long-suffering fans who developed an admirable allegiance to the team in past decades when "respect" and "Patriots" were two words never uttered in the same sentence. But for some old-time fans this season seems an embarrassment of riches. It's good enough to see them win. It might be a little much when they sweep through rival stadiums like Sherman marching through Atlanta on his way to the sea, destroying everything in his wake.

It was unfortunate when this season evolved into that whole "running-up-the-score" debate. Funny how quickly the Patriots went from an American feel-good story to pro football's evil empire. But both of those roles must be played in the passion-play that is the NFL.

The "passion-play" claim can apply to racing, too. It could apply on a larger basis to society in general, as a matter of fact. And it was brought to light in a recent exchange of e-mails I had with a reader of one of my local newspaper columns.

The reader took issue with some remarks I'd made about Thompson Speedway's World Series in October. I'd referred to a local driver who'd crashed in his division's feature. The crash had involved more than one of the division's heavy hitters.

I didn't have much to say about the particular incident that ended the driver's day. The greater point to be made was that the incident had capped off a pretty sloppy race all around. But the reader had written to take me to task for letting the driver in question off the hook. To this person's way of thinking, the driver deliberately crashed into more than one car, intending to put them all out of the race.

That I did not indict the driver for doing so was evidence that I was condoning the driver's actions. To the reader I clearly was on the side of the driver.

I responded that I had no proof the driver had made any deliberate attempt to take anyone out, certainly not from my vantage point at the time. I further stated that I seldom felt I was in a position to direct accusations at racers on the track, being that I was a writer not enjoying the vantage point they might have, the skills they might bring to the task, nor the benefit of rampant adrenalin. I also called into question the motives of the writer, who had chosen to hide behind the cloak of anonymity. As a general rule I pretty much consider worthless any accusation leveled by someone who won't identify themselves or their stake in their claim.

But that's beside the point. What got me riled was the bigger question of why every point of contention today seems to come down to good guy versus bad guy. Why must there always be a villain? I didn't know the guy who'd triggered that crash. I'd interviewed him once; he'd seemed nice enough, although folks looking for good ink tend to act happy to see me.

But I suspected he pretty much was like the rest of us, just another dope looking to make it through the day. I bet the guys he crashed into pretty much were the same. I figured they were really the only ones with a right to beef, and if they had one, they owed it to themselves as well as the guy to take it up with him face to face.

I figure the Pats were running up points because they were paid to do it, and if some defense had a problem with it they had a chance to do something about it every time Brady took a snap. They're just a bunch of dopes, too. So are all those guys racing every week at every track in America.

But some people have a lot to gain by stirring the pot up to get us to hate one guy and love another. Boy, has NASCAR learned how to play that game, and they're printing money doing it. But Carl Edwards was a dope when everyone loved him, and he's a dope now that everyone hates him.

Tony Stewart? Yeah, sure, he's always been a dope. As for me, well, draw your own conclusions.

AFTERMATH

For the Lowell Sun, Attleboro Sun Chronicle *and* Newburyport Daily News, *2000. Both this and the next piece focus upon a pet peeve of mine, as in my day job I work helping survivors of traumatic brain injury return to work.*

Normally after a Winston Cup weekend at New Hampshire International Speedway this column is the place to read about highlights of the weekend that were ignored by a media seemingly focused on finding different ways to tell the same story.

After Kenny Irwin's tragic death in a Winston Cup practice-crash at NHIS Friday, a story about which many fans already feel they've read too much, it nonetheless seems that there are aspects of this story that have yet to be addressed.

Most reporters focused upon the man and the racer who was Kenny Irwin. As they should have. Of course this tragedy took from our midst a supremely-talented young man who was intelligent, personable and had a promising future as a racer.

Coming hard on the heels of Adam Petty's death two months ago literally yards from where Irwin crashed, many reporters described the crash as an ``eery'' or ``tragic'' coincidence and promptly attributed the similarities of these two fatal crashes to fate. Heartfelt eulogies were on everyone's lips. Insightful analysis, on the other hand, has been more elusive.

NASCAR, for its part, also expressed its sympathy for Irwin's family. But Mike Helton also declared that the show had to go on. NASCAR had ``responsibilities.'' Indeed they do.

One would think that number-one among those responsibilities would be insuring that there would be no more crashes like the two already witnessed. Instead NASCAR announced, literally days before the Cup drivers arrived in Loudon, that no conclusive evidence could be found of mechanical failure in Petty's crash and that it was likely no cause ever would be found.

What of the speculation that Petty's throttle had stuck open? It simply was dismissed due to this lack of mechanical evidence. But of course there wasn't mechanical evidence. Any traffic-accident investigator will tell you that it's next to impossible to determine how the controls of crashing cars were deployed due to the pressure placed upon them by the force of the driver thrown forward in a crash. A true investigator therefore looks elsewhere, to skid marks, or to the accounts of eyewitnesses.

Initial eyewitness-reports from the track stated in no uncertain terms that Petty's roaring motor could be heard after he'd lost control. Lacking mechanical evidence that directly disputes these observations, NASCAR should consider these observations the best evidence of what happened rather than suggest that the cause of the crash is not known because there is no mechanical evidence amidst the wreckage to support them.

There also was speculation concerning how the track might be made safer at this hazardous spot. Reports Monday quoted an apparently dismissive track owner Bob Bahre agreeing to make changes if and as specified by NASCAR, but otherwise stating he didn't feel there was anything wrong with his track.

Bahre's statements came off as surprisingly callous, but the Bahres already have demonstrated their concern for the safety and well-being of the competitors at their track. Much of the reason that no pro stock or supermodified races have run at NHIS, two races that would deliver

102

plenty of excitement, is because of the Bahres' worries over the safety of those racers on the big NHIS mile.

This, admittedly, is not the place to suggest what steps might make racing, or Winston Cup cars, or NHIS safer. On the other hand, when you consider how the simple addition of polystyrene barriers has lessoned the impact into the walls of many tracks, and that even the aforementioned supers are equipped with shut-off switches placed above the right toes of their drivers, it's apparent that there are ideas that could be more carefully investigated.

Instead of Bob Bahre stating that foam-barriers explode into a mess when hit, perhaps he could investigate how that might be avoided, or how other materials might also lesson the impact when the wall outside turn-three is hit. Instead of suggesting that an on-off switch would be inadequate, perhaps race-engineers could investigate a more sophisticated system that cuts the engine and applies the brakes if the motor is cranking too fast upon entry into a corner.

This column is written by a writer, not an engineer. Finding a solution is not within a writer's capabilities. But when the question of whether a death like Adam Petty's or Kenny Irwin's can be prevented in the future is answered with a shrug and another comment about the show needing to go on, then drivers who've avoided their own eulogies and families that have not yet needed condolences should demand action.

If this had been a plane crash, no stone would have been left unturned in a quest for the truth. For that matter, if these accidents had occurred in Connecticut, that state's Department of Motor Vehicles would have impounded the cars as part of its own investigation, an investigation on the level of a criminal one.

In New Hampshire it's the lack of such an effort that's criminal.

This follow-up ran in a later column:

A few weeks ago in this column I criticized NASCAR for appearing to avoid the subject of preventing crashes such as those that took the lives of drivers Adam Petty and Kenny Irwin, Jr. Evidence suggested both were propelled into the turn-three wall at New Hampshire International

Speedway by jammed-open throttles.

If I was quick to criticize it's only fair that I give credit to NASCAR for amending tech rules to include the requirements that Winston Cup teams install throttle-stops on their cars as well as engine shut-offs on steering wheels within a thumb's-reach of drivers.

These measures are a start. Still, NASCAR officials need to be a less defensive on this subject (as do certain myopic fans and racing-media members).

AFTER DALE

From the Newburyport Daily News, *2001.*

Normally this would be the last racing column of the season, as our attention turned to the building excitement of the current football season and the first tip-offs and face-offs of winter sports. But this hasn't been a normal racing season, nor, obviously, has it been a normal year.

But the state of racing this season may not be all that big of an issue, anyway. Two tragedies, one on the track at the start of the season and a recent universal one off it, have served to remind us that racing cannot be the sole purpose of a person's life, or even its most important pursuit.

When racing hero Dale Earnhardt died in a last-lap crash in February's Daytona 500 it seemed a greater tragedy than most racefans could imagine. His loss has hung over the entire racing season as fans struggled to come to grips with it and NASCAR struggled to come to grips with its responsibility for it. Yet the tragedy of the September 11 not only forced racing's tragedy into relative insignificance, it inspired us to define our heroes in new and refreshing terms.

It's possible, actually, that these two tragedies share more in common than the simple fact that they happened this year. Consider the aftermath of Earnhardt's death. Remember the reaction of many outsiders to racing? Where in the past there had been much hand-wringing from naysayers about the ``barbarism'' of racing, Earnhardt's death seemed to prompt a sincere outpouring of sympathy as well as universal respect for a man whose legacy had transcended racing. When Earnhardt's driver, Steve Park, won a Winston Cup race and then Earnhardt's Childress Racing replacement Kevin Harvick did the same, sports fans not even into racing appreciated the significance of both victories. Finally, many folks who had looked at racing only with contempt or puzzlement started to get it.

More importantly NASCAR itself finally seems to have come to recognize that it must accept responsibility for protecting drivers. It has often couched its reluctance to do so in vaguely patriotic terms of respecting drivers' freedom. In the world of modern bigtime racing, however, there simply is too much pressure on drivers to forgo their own interests. How as a driver can you justify compromising your performance for your team and your sponsors just to protect yourself?

That question became moot for most drivers by the time NASCAR finally mandated the use of either the HANS or Hutchins device to prevent the hyper extension of the neck that was at least a factor in Earnhardt's death as well as three others last season. Of the regulars competing in Winston Cup only Tony Stewart had not already begun using one of the devices. Surely no one would look to the maturity of Stewart as a model for the most intelligent course of action.

Thus we saw evidence of NASCAR's recognition that it was part of a world much larger than just its own kingdom. And we saw racers recognizing the importance of their roles as husband, father, and folk-figure that were larger than their roles as racecar drivers. All of this, it would seem, is healthy.

Evidently NASCAR could grow still more. The upcoming New Hampshire 300 Winston Cup race the day after Thanksgiving at New Hampshire International Speedway is a case in point. This new date represents a foolish decision that was made after NASCAR got backed into a wall from pressure put on it to postpone or cancel a race it fully intended to run days after the September 11 attacks. We can hope that the race will come off satisfactorily despite the promise of winter approaching. Maybe after that NASCAR will finally accept its role as bigger even than where its own growth has taken them.

Then maybe next season racing will just be fun again. In the meantime this column will return to review that race.

HERE'S WHAT YOU SHOULD DO

From Shorttrack Magazine, *2005. But do they listen?*

I admit that I wouldn't choose to promote a shorttrack if you kidnaped my kids. Who could deal with three or four straight rained-out spring dates after a long winter? Who could accept a crowd so sparse for a weekly show it could share the same hotdog after having a track torn apart by a crowd swollen to the seams for a show presenting demo derbies and spectator drags?

But wait a minute, I didn't start this column to make excuses for promoters. I started it to criticize them. Seriously. See what happens when you give somebody a press-pass and a keyboard?

But here's the deal. Promoters aren't just complaining about smaller crowds these days, they're complaining about *older* crowds, too. Some promoters out there believe this is further evidence that the golden days of shorttrack racing are past, and they only will hang on until these old fans die off. This is where I get testy. It's the job of a promoter to build a track's fan base. That job is ongoing if any track is to survive. And many tracks just aren't doing it.

Promoters and some older fans complain the problem is there are no heroes in racing anymore.

"Where are the new Ollie Silvas, the Bugsys, the Bentleys?" they ask. And yet, there they are, racing every week right under their noses.

You think Bentley Warren built his reputation because he went out and shook everybody's hands, or made commercials? Promoters worked hard to create them. They hosted open shows that were real or made rules that led to outrageous creations. They let drivers fight; hell, they encouraged them, on and off the track.

Go to a baseball or hockey game, even a minor-league one. Read the program. Chances are there's a photo of every player on the team. Biographies provide histories and stats for each player. You can learn how the two teams playing have fared against each other.

Fans will get excited if they can get to know your racers. What do your fans know about them? Your program should include close-ups of drivers, ideally all of them, but at least the top ten or so in each division. Bios should be under the photos. You don't need a life story, but a few blurbs, trading card-style, are a start.

I interviewed Seekonk street-stocker Bob Lantagne for a recent column in the Pawtucket, RI, *Times*. The guy had taken time off from racing to serve in Iraq, for goodness sakes. You think that wouldn't create some rooting interest?

How many drivers at your track are firefighters, or cops? Any teachers? Truck drivers? How about lawyers or Yankee fans? Every track needs its villains. How many put cars together on a wing and a prayer? Folks love underdogs.

You'll also learn much from the PA call of a game. Boy, will the PA announcer pump you up! And you'll be able to actually *hear* it, as well as music chosen specifically to excite the crowd.

Not to pick on anyone specifically, but if Seekonk Speedway wants young fans perhaps they (with apologies to RA Silvia) should retire the 1950s music. The strains of "All the chapel bells were ringing..." won't inspire fans to get excited (To give credit, they also simulcast on local radio. Wear headphones and you know the score).

I know facilities-upkeep is expensive. I guarantee, though, that many tracks have attracted those young families they crave but scared them away after one visit. Rotting benches will do it. Dirt walking paths will, too. Hey, moms wear heels on Saturday night. Bathrooms? My goodness! Can you say "dive?"

Hey, a little paint will do wonders. If you can't pave an area, can you do some landscaping? Yeah, more money to spend. On the other hand, you probably have a dozen competitors who finance their racing by landscaping. Could you trade for advertising? Or is there a vocational or agricultural school around? While you're at it, put up a playground. Keep mom and the kids happy and Dad'll be happy, too.

Just make your track a comfortable place to be. There's a drive-in theater where I live. Mid-afternoons there already are scores of movie-goers there, enjoying picnics or buying food while flinging frisbees around. Could they do that at your track?

You've heard – and said – a million times that people have more to do today than ever. What are folks doing instead of coming to the races? Find out. Go to a ball game. Go to the park. Find the people. Figure out what the attraction is. Give kids a fighting chance to be gray-haired old fans at your racetrack 50 years from now, buying a ticket from your kid, with grandkids in tow behind.

THIS IS YOUR BRIAN ON RACING

From Late Model Racer, *2017. In addition to writing about racing, I"ve spent 30 years helping people with traumatic brain injury return to employment.*

We can thank football for reminding us that our brains are more than just body-parts. The controversy surrounding recent head injuries in the National Football League recalls the debate over head injuries racing experienced years ago after Dale Earnhardt was killed. Ultimately NASCAR responded positively. No young driver ever would drive at over 200 mph wearing an open-face helmet and a pair of shades.

Can the same be said of our favorite weekend warriors? Can the same be said of you? Are you using your brain to keep it safe?

If you are, then you likely understand why the brain is more fragile and complex than, say, a rib or your arm. Of course, it controls heartbeat and breathing and every other life-sustaining function in your body. More than that, and of interest to any racer, it controls the functions, such as reflexes, reaction and judgement, that separate the fast guys from the slow ones.

That being the case, it's obvious why a brain injury can be devastating. To understand a less obvious tragedy of a brain-injury, though, you need to know a little about how the brain works. So bear with us, here.

Your brain actually is made up of a lot of different sections. Yeah, they all work together, but each performs a specific job all its own.

The brain-stem, where vital functions are controlled and the senses and reflexes are coordinated, is situated in a fairly safe spot, connecting the center of the brain to the spinal cord below it. The cerebellum, which coordinates the movements you control as well as your balance, is also relatively safe, in the back of the skull about level with the ears.

The most exposed sections of your brain make up the cortex. They basically fill up the top of your skull. The cortex is divided in two different ways. First, it's split into left and right hemispheres, each directing the opposite side of the body. One side also controls speech and learning and is believed to determine if a person is left or right-handed. The other side is believed to influence artistic and creative skills. The cortex is also divided into sections called lobes. No, not like on a cam. The senses, though coordinated in the brain-stem, are controlled by three of these lobes in the rear two-thirds of the skull. The info collected here is processed and then gets stored as memory.

Knowing what each of these parts of the brain does can give you a hint to how someone will be affected by a brain injury – if it's known what areas of the brain were damaged. If the brain's frontal lobes are involved, however, all bets are off. That's because your personality is created and controlled in this vulnerable area.

"The frontal lobe controls how people behave; how they respond to the world," explains Dr. Frank Sparadeo, who, as a neuropsychologist, has decades of experience studying the relationship between the brain and behavior. "We call it 'executive function.' It's the ability to make judgements or to plan ahead. It's also the ability to reason, control impulses and assess risks."

Assess risks, eh?

"The frontal lobe is the area of the brain affected by alcohol," Sparadeo offers, "so if you think about the part of the personality suppressed by alcohol, those are the same functions affected by a frontal-lobe injury."

That's scary enough, but a change in personality isn't the only effect of a frontal lobe injury.

"Recognizing new limits imposed by any injury is always difficult," explains Sally Hay, who as a clinical socialworker made a career of treating survivors of traumatic brain-injury, "and an injury to the head is among the most devastating psychologically. Frequently combined with a loss of judgement, this can lead to totally unrealistic expectations for recovery on the part of a head-injury survivor."

Obviously a major ability-deficit, and the inability to see it, can lead to a major disaster on a racetrack. But minor deficits worry Sparadeo just as much.

"One of the most difficult things for people to deal with," he explains, "is that many manifestations of a brain-injury are not visible. A victim may seem just fine but have trouble with the simplest things."

These troubles can be difficult to spot. The doctors might be experts, but they can't know how much a person's abilities and personality have been affected by a brain injury if they didn't know the person before the injury. So if it seems apparent that a racer intends to go back to racing, the specialists can only assess the obvious mental and physical functions. A driver's judgement or split-second decision-making ability often cannot truly be assessed until he's back on the track.

All of this can be pretty sobering, but if you've gone out and bought a modern, top-of-the-line helmet, you probably figure you've got yourself covered. You might be – until you wear it. There are no guarantees after that. That's because helmets are almost as fragile as the part of the body they're designed to protect. And they have to be, because if they weren't, they wouldn't work.

The two most important parts of a helmet are the shell and the liner. The liner is not the foam padding on the inside of the helmet; that's just there for comfort. The liner is between that and the shell. It's made of expanded polystyrene, which is that white foam they use for cheap coffee cups.

That stuff, not the shell, is what saves your brain when your head sustains an impact. It does it by absorbing the blow passed to it by the shell. What the shell does is distribute the load over as wide an area of the liner as possible. It also, of course, resists penetration by sharp or flying objects. The key words here are 'absorb' and 'distribute.' To do their jobs, these components basically are crushed, cracked and otherwise destroyed. On big impacts they suck it up bigtime. But on smaller ones this self-destruction may not even be visible. This is why, by the way, a safety helmet for racing wouldn't work for football players. They would need a new helmet virtually every play.

Any impact your helmet may sustain affects it to some extent. So does a lot of other stuff. If you've ever seen anyone put gas or a solvent in one of those foam coffee-cups, you can imagine what even fumes can do to a helmet's liner, which is made of the same material. The helmet's shell is affected as well. How much any one helmet is affected is impossible to guess. Certainly after a major impact you should kiss your helmet to thank it and then kiss it goodbye. But even a minor impact should make you suspicious.

Fortunately throwing it away isn't your only option. After any significant impact you can send your helmet back to the manufacturer or its representative. They will advise you if it's serviceable and repair it if they can. This is a free service and is offered by most reputable helmet manufacturers, who, after all, have a stake in your survival.

Many times the only reason drivers buy a helmet is in response to new standards from Snell, a private foundation that tests and rates helmets. Most sanctioning bodies require drivers to wear Snell-approved helmets. Snell's standard, considered the highest in the industry, approves helmets on a five-year basis. Helmets with a 2015 rating would meet the most recent standards.

But there's more to it than that. Snell further breaks their ratings down into 'M' and 'SA' standards. M standards are set for motorcycle use, where the wearer is concerned not only with impact but with the abrasion involved in breathtaking 90-mph skids along pavement. SA or "special application" standards address more issues, including those of concern to short-track racers, such as fire and multiple impacts.

There are instances where no helmet can protect you from a brain-injury. Medical history has documented that, and there's no way around it. A helmet protects your head, but it can't help if you stop breathing or your heart stops. The resulting lack of oxygen to the brain can cause permanent brain-damage in a matter of minutes. In that case, only someone well-trained in CPR can help. So who makes up the safety-crew at your track? Inquiring brains should want to know.

Sparadeo notes one other possible cause of brain-damage which is much less obvious but can be just as dangerous. In fact, it's what killed Earnhardt.

"Even if you don't hit your head, your brain can sustain damage. If your body stops quickly upon impact, your brain will continue to move forward inside your skull. Not only do these deceleration-injuries stretch the brain-stem, but your brain can actually impact upon the inside of your skull."

Which actually is a pretty rough surface.

"These impacts can be minor," he cautions, "but after a few years the effect can be cumulative. After years of this, is a driver's judgement as good as it was before? This is an open question."

A driver's personality can change as well.

"Race drivers are notorious for their eccentricities," says Sparadeo, who, it should be noted, is a pretty enthusiastic car guy, "but I have a hunch at least some of the older guys might have changed subtly due to repeated minor head-injuries over the years."

There are steps you can take to minimize your chance of a head injury. First of all, love your helmet. Invest in a bag or case for it, and in general treat it with TLC. If you have any suspicions at all about its condition, send it back to the factory for testing. Better yet, replace it. Good helmets are admittedly expensive, but what's your head worth?

Make sure the new one fits and that it won't interfere with business when you get behind the wheel. Pay attention to other pieces of equipment that can prevent or possibly contribute to head injuries. Head-restraints and neck-collars reduce the possibility of deceleration-injuries. Good rollbar padding can augment the performance of your helmet. Better yet, position rollbars so there's less chance of your head hitting them in the first place.

Just take precautions, check out your equipment, and get the best.

In short, use your head.

114

KIDDIE CARS

From Shorttrack Magazine, 2005. The young driver to whom I refer in this piece? He didn't make it anywhere near Nextel Cup – or whatever name they've given it since then.)

They say Mozart wrote his first symphony when he was seven months old, pounding the first movement out on one of those colorful little xylophones that the French forerunner of Fisher-Price used to make. Okay, maybe not, but the composer long has served as the model of the childhood prodigy.

Mozart, who lived a few hundred years ago, was rare to the point that he's still serving our popular mythology, but today childhood prodigies are everywhere. Sports, far from being the exception, seems to be actively cultivating them, having recognized their value as marketing tools to help foist frivolous products upon the youthful masses ever lustful for new diversions.

Racing, sad to say, is not immune. Worse, many of the people you would hope would protect kids from this nonsense seem to be willingly complicit in their promotion. Last season I witnessed the parent of a talented kid trolling for contacts in the pits during a major race weekend. The parent was trying to dig a pipeline that would lead out of New England and south to feed the monstrous machine of (then) Nextel Cup racing. This parent admitted the son's adventure in one of the region's touring series had ended badly. Yet despite this a deal was in the works that would put the kid in an even more competitive series.

The question of whether this boy might have been better off taking a step down into a series where he might qualify on a regular basis, the better to learn the rather important art of racing with others, not only did not get answered, it didn't even get asked. There was no point. The clock was ticking. Time was running out. The kid needed to be moving on, and up. A step backwards was a step into oblivion, a concession that the path to stardom had ended, that the kid was washed up, over the hill – at 17.

No matter that the one thing the kid could do that would garner attention, namely win, wasn't being accomplished on any level. Worse, the kid wasn't even getting a chance to demonstrate the ability to learn about his competition and figure out precisely how they could be beaten, another skill of some value.

There's a bigger issue here, though. Recently *Shorttrack* Senior Editor Chris Romano informed me that a 15-year-old kid had crashed a late model during a practice-day down south. He got out of shape in a corner, and rather than collect himself, as maturity might have dictated (it was, after all, just practice), he reportedly lost the car completely while trying to hang on to it. The car rammed into the wall and caught fire. The fact that the track in question had not mandated adequate fire equipment is a point for another day, but this kid lost his life as his father and grandfather suffered serious burns in a futile attempt to save him.

Certainly this is the most horrific price a racer can pay. Some would argue that it's one not worth paying. But, that argument aside as well, is a 15-year-old kid in a position to understand even the lesser stakes of this particular game?

We have middle-school kids banking every bit of their fiber on getting one of maybe 50 jobs that exist as drivers in Nextel Cup, and most are that specific about their goal. Even in the rarified air of NBA basketball there are ten times as many opportunities. And in basketball college is a part of the process of making it, even if many basketball players choose not to complicate the process by actually going to class. Hey, that's their choice, and they're adults by the time they make it.

116

These kids and their parents are hitching on to a star that likely exists as nothing more than the light it's casting. The fire is light-years away. And not "might be" light-years away. This observer, here, right now, will say to every childhood racing-prodigy reading this column unequivocally that you WILL NOT MAKE IT to Nextel Cup.

Sure, I might be wrong about once every ten years. Where's that leave you?

KIDDIE CARS II

From Trackside Magazine, *2002. Another pet peeve, evidently.*

The modern world of sports is crawling with child prodigies. At the same points in their lives where today's middle-agers were playing three-on-three hockey on the neighborhood pond, shooting at winter-boot goals, today's youthful hockey players join travel teams and attend camps run by former NHLers. Basketball players who have yet to shave are courted (excuse the pun) by colleges and athletic-shoe companies. Football players who aren't allowed to ride their bicycles outside their neighborhood are playing for national championships.

Auto racing is no exception. When I was a kid I fulfilled my racing fantasies in 1/32 scale, racing homebuilt specials in the basements and attics of my friends. Forget Dad building a quarter-midget for me. My family was lucky when it had a lawnmower that ran decently. Thus the lawn got the grooming, not the son. But now every kid who dreams of being a Winston Cup driver has a quarter midget in the garage that is as exotic as the Indy Cars I was trying to replicate in clear plastic and soldered brass. The hand-painted helmets they slide on to their sugar-plum-filled heads duplicate quarter-sized paint schemes, the better to shine from the pages of homemade sponsorship proposals cobbled together using term-paper techniques. But hey, this is serious business.

Far be it from me to dash these pint-sized plans against the rocks of reality. There are worse dreams to entertain than one of making a career in racing. Beside, from the masses of self-absorbed children who strut their stuff at Sugar Hill and the Little-T will come tomorrow's touring champions. Unfortunately by the looks of it by then there will be no living with them when that day comes.

I see a lot of these kids in action. I visit the Little-T regularly; hey, slick racecars are slick racecars and always are a treat to check out. I still pop in from time to time on tracks where I once raced karts, and at places like Pomfret and Woodstock there are more kids racing than ever.

Tracks such as Seekonk, Beech Ridge and Londonderry have distinct divisions for kids. I'm not above watching these young racers get their mistakes out of their systems.

Among all these little-league racecar drivers are a fair number of very talented children. Some are demonstrating grown-up skills, and they're proving it by taking advantage of special dispensations extended by area shorttracks to outrun full-sized competitors in full-sized cars. These are the sport's prodigies, and these particular boys and girls are earning the right to entertain those plans for stardom realistically.

I've been in contact this season with at least one parent of such a prodigy. His son simply ate up the competition at at least two tracks running his particular brand of junior-size racer and his dad wants to get the word out. On at least one occasion I was happy to oblige. The family lived in a town covered by a daily paper for which I write and the son's record truly was newsworthy.

Dad was not coy about his interest in spreading the word about his son. In fact early this winter he contacted me to find out how he more effectively could publicize his son's success. I provided the usual advice about developing a mailing list of media outlets with legitimate potential interest and the need to keep releases and photos noteworthy, professional and easy to utilize. Good advice for anyone looking to do the same, incidently.

In the meantime we have been party to the spectacle that has been

119

the Winston-Cup-championship season of one young Tony Stewart. Stewart is one in a line of young racers who have "arrived" via the path to glory discussed here. Certainly Stewart amply demonstrated the effectiveness of this path in developing a racer's track skills. It seems, though, that his behavior has revealed that this path to glory has the potential to become a road to ruin just a readily.

We are not here to conduct any Stewart bashing. That is too easy and it would constitute a simplistic look at an apparently complex man. Besides, I like Tony Stewart. Sure, he acts like a major-league jerk sometimes. But it seems that, if his misbehavior has not exactly been justified, it at least has been instigated by outside actions. Spend a day observing how many Cup fans treat their heroes and you'll come away in awe of how patient and accommodating these guys can be. I've seen any number of acts by fans that deserved a hostile response. Many fans are major-league jerks themselves.

Rather, the point here is that if you look at the career of a racecar driver in totality and you begin to realize that the reality is much less dazzling than the fantasy many of these children maintain. More importantly, this is a fantasy that will become reality for only a tiny fraction of those aspire to it. All who do, on the other hand, will become adults in this society. Whether they grow up to become racers should be secondary to that. So every effort should be made to ensure that they don't mature with the belief that theirs was a life predetermined but rather that they, simply, were damned lucky.

Thinking about all of this made me realize that there was more valuable advice I could offer this dad than how to develop a press-campaign. And I believe it would be good advice for many parents out there as they try to give their kids chances to turn their dreams into reality. So parents and guardians, here's what I feel you can do – should do – for your young aspiring racecar stars.

First, make them realize that their chosen occupation is intrinsically trivial. With all the disease in this world, with the poverty, the injustice, the terror, the hunger, the inhumanity, they are directing their lives to one of its most self-absorbed pursuits. Worse, any sport simply is a contrived exercise with little practical value to humanity. While others are curing diseases, keeping people safe, creating jobs   or providing basic human needs, your child will be driving a car in circles for hundreds of miles to no productive end beyond entertainment. To such an unproductive result they likely will devote almost all of their waking hours. This does not mean there is no honor in racing, but there is only if a racer can maintain a passion for the sport that is equally all-consuming. Don't ever confuse your dreams with your kid's. Yours will not support what will be required of them, only theirs will.

Secondly, you need to make it clear to them that odds are they will not make it. Many are called but few are chosen to make a career as a racecar driver. Don't expect it will happen. Yes, they must work hard. Yes, they must sacrifice many of the joys of youth to this seriously grown-up quest. Yes, of course, they must be good. But all of these things comprise only the entry-requirements for a shot at the top. The two or three percent who succeed possess only a bit more of these qualities than the 98 percent who fail – sometimes not even as much. And despite what the athletic-shoe ad might have proclaimed, it says here that you shouldn't try if you are *not* prepared to fail.

Don't expect anyone to be impressed. Guys, most girls don't care. In fact racing will ask much more of them as opposed to what they will get back than it ever will ask of you. And girls, guys more than likely will be intimidated, not impressed, by your racing. Kids need to find their own satisfaction in racing. It's too lonely of an effort to do it for any other reason.

Make sure your kid maintains some self-respect and some perspective. Any of today's ``sexy'' occupations, sports star, rock star, movie star, TV star, endures 1,000 wannabes for each serious and successful player. Most every wannabe is willing to do whatever it takes to become a star. Why, even among motorsports journalists I've been witness to this phenomenon, especially with televsion. There are hordes of writers who will do anything to get down to Charlotte so they can do a gig on Speed Channel. There are a few who bother the producer of the cable-based race program I work on every time they see him. For shame, because I have no intention of moving to Charlotte. A couple of these folks have been like bosom buddies to my face but insist on selling themselves as better choices than me to do my gig. There's no shame in ambition, but the ambition of some knows no shame.

Teach your kids to be nice. It's a racer's most marketable commodity, for one thing, but it's more basic than that. Don't let them become so full of themselves that they think they're better than anyone. They're not doing anything important, for one thing, remember? That autograph seeker probably provides a more essential service to society than they do. And the reporter asking a stupid question might know it's stupid but also might realize it's a reporter's job to get the answer from the source, not speculate about how the source might answer.

Love racing. This is the only reason to race, for you or your kid. The further your child progresses that more racing will become like work. How many racers have proclaimed they're only comfortable in their racecars? That's no line. Most every other part of the job gets to stink.

Again, only passion will support the necessary effort. And with that passion intact whatever level of success your child achieves will prove to be sufficient.

BIG BLOCKS

From the Attleboro Sun Chronicle, 2002.

The dictionary defines the word super as ``in excessive intensity or degree,'' which makes it easy to understand the title ``supermodified.''

Many race fans find excessively intense as being the perfect description of a supermod race at a place like Star Speedway. For that matter, some folks find simply looking at a Super excessively intense. And why not? A super's tires alone can intimidate. You could use a super to *pave* your racetrack, before this psycho-steamroller went out and tore all your new pavement up. And the surface plane of a winged super has enough square footage to lift a Piper Cub full of portly trade-show reps fresh from a free buffet.

And then there are those engines. Hanging off its host's left-side frame-rail, a super's big-block looks every bit up to the task of providing emergency power to a public-housing complex. Talk about excessively intense. We are, after all, referring to the most powerful powerplant found anywhere in shorttrack racing.

There was a time (``not so long ago,'' as the folklorists are fond of saying) when big-blocks in race cars weren't such a big deal. They were more like the norm. NASCAR's Grand National series, the precursor to today's trademarked Winston Cup series, used to circle the race tracks of the South motivated by big-block power. Closer to home, supermods are an evolution of plain-ole mods. Back in the days of iron men and wooden race cars (okay, let's say ``iron men and angle-iron race cars) modifieds were powered as often as not by big-blocks.

What happened to drop big-block race engines from favor? Blame the fuel shortage of the early 1970s, for a start. It forced NASCAR to shift to small-block power for political reasons as much as anything. For everyone else it was an even simpler equation. When the automotive manufacturers stopped putting production big-blocks in their land yachts and light trucks it was the beginning of the end for the supply of the basic building-block to big-block racing power.

These days, after 30 years of development, small-block engines make as much power as the big-blocks did back in days of yore. To some that conjures up the metaphor of the supermod as dinosaur, as comically obsolete as a brontosaurus with a desk job. Why, even Star has shifted to supers racing under small-block power, a move that rejuvenated open-wheel racing at the southern New Hampshire quarter-mile oval.

But the move to small-blacks in shorttrack racing has come at a cost – literally. A competitive small-block engine in some divisions costs what the typical house cost back in the days of big-blocks. And they can demand as much attention as a petulant grandchild.

Rick Wentworth is one guy who would know. He grew up immersed in supermod racing. As a kid he was a regular in the shop of supermodified legend Ollie Silva, who garaged his car in Wentworth's neighborhood. So did Mike Ordway in later years. Wentworth became a valued member of Ordway's pit crew and watched from the pits as Ordway won a title at Star in 1984.

When Wentworth decided to go racing himself he purchased a Vic Miller-built super, installed a mildly-tweaked smallblock V-8, and drove to Hudson Speedway's 350-Supermod Rookie of The Year title in 1997. He also won the 350 feature that became part of Star's famous supermod ``Classic'' that season. Then he followed up that performance with the 350-Super title in '98 as the division moved to Star full-time.

124

Two years ago he admitted that if big-block supers had been the only option available to him when he started driving he likely never would have been able to do it. The 350s were an alternative he could afford. These days, though, it's possible he wouldn't be able to get rolling at all.

``The price of the small-blocks has gotten out of hand,'' he maintains. ``They're just as expensive as a big-block to repair as far as components go. There's a lot of expensive parts going into them now.''

Big-blocks, on the other hand, can be the family dogs of racing. While Wentworth believes building a front-running ISMA big-block still is a daunting expense, last season he was able to purchase an ex-Vic Miller big-block for under ten grand to mate to his Miller chassis. He then drove his new combination to 14th in the Star Classic and tenth at Thompson Speedway.

His racing curtailed by a commitment to going through the firefighting academy full-time, he's invested extra time this season in rebuilding his new mill. But that's the only extra investment he's made.

``I'm paying the same amount of money to freshen it up as I would the small-block,'' he says.

The idea of racing a big-block as an economy measure is not a new one, actually. In fact, there's reason to believe it's why mods started running them in the first place. Ray Belanger's ever-growing collection of vintage modifieds includes a couple of big-blocks, including the XC-1, purported to be the original big-block mod. Indeed, the number ``XC-1'' stands for ``Experimental Chevy-One.''

Belanger believes the XC-1 was conceived as a big-track car.

``They were looking for a lot of power,'' he says, ``and cheap.''

Power was easy to find in the motor driving the XC-1 as well as Belanger's other big-block mod, Will Cagle's old number 24, which supposedly was the craftwork of Lennie Boehler.

Belanger drove the gleaming white 24 at Seekonk once. ``It was unbelievable!'' he marvels of its raw power.

``You just needed a big cam and a *big* carburetor,'' he laughs. ``And the headers on this thing. You can stick your head in them. When I start it in the garage it shakes everything off the walls. It's like a big bass drum. The small blocks are like snare drums.''

That sound of two dozen of these bass drums pounding out a rhythm as they rocket around a shorttrack is one that must be experienced. But maybe that experience doesn't have to be limited to supermod fans. All of the factors that drove big-blocks from racing seem to have receded like Jimmy Spencer's hairline, under a toupee of discretionary income. The auto manufacturers are stuffing bigger and bigger engines into SUVs that are large enough to block out the sun. Those engines are designed with a level of sophistication unheard of in the aforementioned days of yore.

Imagine, if you will, a modified powered by the V-10 out of a Dodge Viper, and you might wonder if history is ready to repeat itself. Could the time have arrived for some farseeing car builder to create the XC-2?

ONLY THERE FOR THE CRASHING

From Trackside Magazine, *2002. You'll no longer see sportswriters belittle motor racing. Now it's just ignored. As for newspapers...*

I saw one again. One of those "They're only there to see the crashing" stories in a newspaper. I'm sure you've seem them, too. Invariably they categorize us as a bunch of flaming yahoos interested only in seeing blood flow and racecars burn.

This particular one wasn't in a daily paper, though (wasn't "even" would be a better way to put it). It was in a neighborhood monthly, August's Eastside Monthly, as in the trendy East Side in Providence, R.I. My wife, Jan, had picked it up to kill some time while in Providence waiting for an after-work meeting. She brought it to me knowing I'd have an interest in seeing it.

Usually, these stories infuriate me, as I believe professional sportswriters should know better. Professionals should do their jobs, cover the sport of racing because their readers want to follow it, and not question its validity as a sport simply because they don't like it or understand it.

Why, the usually professional Bob Ryan of the *Boston Globe* once wrote a column precisely about how he didn't understand racing.

127

Funny, I always read his columns to learn what he knows, not what he doesn't. It's difficult to be impressed by people who brag about their ignorance. That's something you confess, not declare.

The writer in question here didn't brag about his ignorance, he just revealed it. But it didn't infuriate me – for two reasons. For one thing, there was nothing professional about his ignorant column. No interviews, no insights, nothing but his drivel. But there was a bigger reason I was able to dismiss this idiotic excuse for journalism.

One of the points this gentleman made in his piece concerned how the fans at the race he attended at Thompson Speedway (which he made clear was the only race he'd ever attended) sat quietly during races and would only make noise when there was a crash. This was portrayed as if the crowd sat boringly staring into space waiting for the sound of squealing tires and tearing metal. Well, it happened that I'd attended a race at Thompson the Thursday evening before this piece was handed to me, and I'd made some observations about the crowd myself. These observations – and this crowd – had so impressed me that I'd already decided this was something I wanted to share with you.

Amid my duties on behalf of magazines, newspapers and TV, which compel me to work from pits or press box, I'm apt to head to a track in my neck of the woods simply to enjoy the show and witness an evening's racing without meeting specific requirements such as taping openings or catching up with drivers while the show goes on around me. This was one of those nights. It was a Thursday when I had no other engagements, so with Thompson minutes away from home I fired up the bike, blasted over the hills separating home and the track, and headed in to settle among the crowd.

I'm a people-watcher wherever I am. Any crowd is interesting for the peculiar examples of humanity it contains. This one at Thompson was no exception. But I began to notice some things about the crowd that in three-and-a-half decades of going to races I'd never really noticed before. Like the fact that people sat quietly during a race. But that's the one similarity between what I and our opinionated ignoramus saw. For what I noticed with this crowd was precisely how it watched the race quietly. The fans might have been quiet, but most were focusing intently. Heads rotated with the rotating racecars. Some fans obviously were focused on the action right at the front of the field. Some focused toward the back of the lines of racecars, evidently interested in personal friends or favorites. But there were few fans not intently directing their attention to some portion of the race in front of them.

Some in groups would occasionally be seen motioning with their hands, performing the flying hands routine. You've seen that one often enough. Two hands held out, palms down, sweeping through the air as two cars would sweep through a corner, one hand cutting downward to imitate a noteworthy move on the track. Other hands pointed toward certain cars in gestures of excitement or insight. Heads frequently came close together as messages were conveyed over the roar of engines.

Ah, yes, the roar of engines. Of course people weren't cheering. They had enough brains to figure out that it's sort of pointless to root on a driver in a roaring racecar. I figured that out before I graduated from childhood.

And did they react when there was a crash on the track? Did they make a lot of noise? Yes, they made plenty of noise. I wouldn't say that what I noticed was cheering, though. There were shrieks and gasps and shouts, and people yelled as if large insects had suddenly flew into their faces. But to me cheering sounds unique. It's a sound of joy, of happy exhilaration. What I heard that night conveyed excitement, but joy? I've been in the stands when the Pats scored a touchdown, or when the Sox scored a run. Or, for that matter, when a fight broke out during a Bruins game. I know what cheering sounds like.

I did witness some mocking enjoyment of on-track mayhem, admittedly. This was no surprise. It came during Thompson's mini stock races. Yet the mayhem unique to mini stocks is, as all regular racefans know, generally harmless and often quite comical. You know the stuff. One car carving its own unusual line around the track, one that inevitably leads to failure. One driver trying to hang on to a car he doesn't know he's already lost. This is the stuff of a field of drivers trying to get a clue. Some eventually will find it, and fans will enjoy the process of a previously ignorant racer learning and growing in a demanding craft. Others are doomed to suffer ignominiously in front of this crowd before they slink away quietly. Credit them for trying.

I came away from the race that evening with a sense of respect for the fans on hand to see that show. It seemed obvious to me that this was not a horde of yahoos, but a group of folks knowledgeable, opinionated and involved in their sport.

"Gee," I thought to myself, "anybody you brought to a race would be able to see that there was more going on here than a bunch of guys going around in circles while everybody waited for some of them to crash."

I guess I was wrong.

OUT OF MY LEAGUE

From Trackside Magazine, 1999 *Since this was written, all those newspaper jobs have dried up for both Paul and myself, New Hampshire International Speedway is now New Hampshire* Motor Speedway, *and there aren't as many of those ravenous fans at NASCAR races. I blame NASCAR .*

Oh, and "one of New England's major papers" was the Boston Globe.

Something dawned on me during my recent visit to New Hampshire International Speedway to cover the Winston Cup]iffy Lube 300.

It wasn't a revelation; it came over me more slowly than that. The more I worked, the more I watched, the more of this entire event I witnessed, the more I realized it. What I began to realize is that perhaps my well-documented ambivalence about the version of my favorite sport that is the obsession of most racefans may not be a reflection of what it lacks. It may be a reflection of what I lack.

If you know me, you know I can't accept this easily. I still think I'm perfect. So what is it that leads me to think this way?

I love racing. Even after over 30 years as a fan it still has the power to make me get giddy with excitement. But it's been a long time since a Winston Cup race got me giddy. This year's]iffy Lube 300 was an interesting race, but it didn't get me giddy.

And yet racing did get me giddy over the course of the weekend. I got giddy at rustic Pines Speedway when two crusty dirt Modifieds stayed side-by-side as they slid through two comers that I would have swom were much too narrow for such foolishness. I got giddy over the rumor that the PRO Tour for Trucks' Phil Rowe might be trying to put together a similar tour for Pro Stocks. He's conceivably a guy who might actually be able to make it work! Maybe! Now that's a pretty flimsy piece of information to get excited about. I "must" love racing.

Actually I began to wonder if maybe I was in the wrong place as I began to help set up the tent-trailer I regularly stay in at NHIS. My host is brother John, up to take photos. With us is our younger brother Paul, who will file daily reports for the *Metrowest Daily News*. We've made this trip for every Cup race at NHIS. The first time, John and I set up tents on the edge of a parking lot and took showers by dumping buckets of cold water over each other. When he got the camper we thought we were styling.

Friday we found a spot in the area reserved for competitors and workers and began to pop up the pop-up. It's a beauty, a classic really. In much the same way that the "Checkered FIag Announcer" Gremlin *Trackside* Field Rep Rick Mariscal currently drives to racetracks is a classic. But when Paul flipped up the bar that supports the tent over one of the extended beds, I heard a rip that sounded like a pair of jeans being tom apart. By the time we were done flipping the bar back down we had a foot-long tear in the actual, original, vintage canvas.

I was shocked. We do try to keep the camper original, and it's lovingly cared for. Why, we'd just installed a new wiring-hamess we'd bought at Benny's onto the trailer weeks before, retaining only the original, vintage taillights. Sure, they didn't work very well, but at least we'd preserved the vintage appearance. After this, though, I was beginning to wonder if John's $300 had been a bad investment six years ago.

Others, however, made better investments. We were surrounded, as was usual, by giant motorhomes and trailers. Some of them could be counted on later to run generators to power TVs or some other comfort of home while we read trade papers passed out in the media center (which doesn't take too long once you realize they all publish the exact same press-releases and photos).

At least this weekend it wouldn't be hot. When it was hot some generators ran all night as their owners slept in air-conditioned comfort. We, on the other hand, camped.

With the tarpaulin we normally set up outside the camper we covered the end that sustained the damage. Then we gathered what we needed to go to work and headed into the NHIS infield and pit area. Our first stop usually is the track's media center. There we grab lockers for photo gear, books and other items that are tough to carry around. While Paul claims a site to set up his laptop for forwarding reports to his paper, I head toward the garages to see who's already having a tough weekend.

My mission is different than Paul's. While he will file Winston Cup news reports, my iob is to contribute pieces to three newspapers: the Lowell (Mass.) *Sun*, the Attleboro (Mass.) *Sun Chronicle*, and the Norwich (Conn.) *Bulletin*. By the time anyone reads these pieces they'll know who won. Hopefully these stories will tell them some things they didn't know.

Admittedly, then, I'm often not where a reporter would need to be. While they need to talk to the fast guys I might be more interested in what some slow guy has to say. This is getting harder. Security will tolerate you when you're part of a mass of reporters. Go somewhere different and evidently they figure you don't know what you're doing. And I admit that no one is going to give me the best-dressed reporter award. For that I'd be competing against what has become a pervasive polo-shirt-and-Dockers ensemble that doesn't quite work for me. We won't even get into haircuts.

Don't expect me to change in this area, for it has its advantages, too. At a CART race I eavesdropped on a post-race discussion as Emerson Fittipaldi complained passionately to Roger Penske that the mishandling of his pit stops had cost him a race won by teammate Al Unser. I also overheard as a media rep for Penske instructed a reporter from one of New England's major papers to report that Emmo was upset about his tires, which indeed had blistered early in the race. The reporter did so. I, instead, had a story nobody else had.

On the other hand, it was kind of embarrassing one time when Kyle Petty, leaving his car on pit lane after qualifying, reached for my pen and pad to give me an autograph.

This year, though, there was no opportunity for that. While TV crewmembers crowded around each driver as he walked from his car after his qualifying run, a security official shooed me away, refusing to give me an explanation of why. Now I had to chase any driver from whom I wanted a comment as they headed toward their trailer. This amounted to a crapshoot. There always was the chance that the next driver out would do something even more noteworthy than the guy you'd chased.

Television gets this sort of special treatment all weekend. You come to realize that at a NASCAR race TV is not just another news medium, it's actually part of the production. That may seem obvious. What isn't quite as obvious is that, as part of the production, TV always is in danger of rejecting hard truths in the pursuit of a good show.

There are plenty of people who are supposed to be there to cover the show who really want to be part of it. Others want to take home part of it. Some people hang around in the media center the entire weekend, munching on the free cookies and talking much too loudly.

You can get toys, too. When someone went around passing out pins Sunday, one person kept asking for another pin – four times. Another media-type returned to his briefcase repeatedly, stuffing a new free ballcap into it each time.

Some of these people don't leave the media center, even during the race. I'm beginning to understand that, though. Unless you make the trek up to the track's pressbox, there is no good place for press members to watch the race. I'd always preferred to roam the pits during races, again on the prowl for a behind-the-scenes morsel of news. Now pit road is as crowded as the mall on Christmas Eve, except that none of the crowd is particularly interested in doing anything other than standing there. Nobody, that is, except crewmembers.

What they put up with and how they handle it rate awards for patience. They'll keep their cool while moving hundreds of pounds of equipment through this sea of racefans. Who can blame them if there's just a hint of impatience when they say, "excuse me," repeatedly to people oblivious to the fact that they're in the middle of a particularly hazardous worksite?

Even more ignorant are the folks who camp out on top of this equipment. They'll stand on pit carts - or even on stacks of tires. One guy was observed as he removed a tire from one carefully-matched stack so his woman would have a place to sit!

Trying to roam the pits under these conditions is like running down Wall Street on a Monday morning. It's interesting, too, that those same folks who don't notice somebody pulling a cart with three gas cans through this mess will bolt out of the way for TV's pit reporters and the cameras that follow. NASCAR tolerates this. Certainly the measured patience of crews comes by way of directives from NASCAR itself.

Does the fact that I don't understand make me elitist, or conversely, naive? I know racing is special because of its accessibility to its fans. But so much of it is forced; so much is faked. There are so many drivers who seem like great guys on TV. Yet they blow off anyone without a camera or an autograph-request. There again TV ends up creating a reality instead of revealing it. (For the record, my experience suggests that Jeff Gordon, as well as Kyle Petty, Jimmy Spencer, Jeff Burton and John Andretti, to name a few, are not among these fakes. Dale Eamhardt is not exactly charming, but you know that. He is no fake.)

I did find a place to see the race and, armed with stopwatch and radio, was able to get the job done. And if I don't know if I can play the NASCAR Winston Cup game, I do know one thing; I know where Tony Stewart disappeared after the race.

WHAT'S UP WITH RACING

From Shorttrack Magazine, *2005*

Things have gotten out of hand.
It used to be that you built a racecar following a few rules and then you showed up with your creation to do battle against a bunch of guys who had done the same. It was fair way to compete on the racetrack.

No more. Not with the bulging pocketbooks that some car builders bring to the table. Nowadays it's gotten to the point that racing is more a measure of the money in the bank than it is the talent in the garage. You have divisions where you can tell before the racing even starts who's going to win – as well as who's hopelessly outclassed – by looking at the haulers. Go to a super race and watch as the guys with the big haulers run away and hide from the guys in the little ones.

That's why I love a series like ACT. Nothing fancy about an ACT car. One pretty much looks the same as the other. And the beauty of that is more than skin-deep. Why, these guys all are running the exact same crate engine. Their shocks are restricted, too. But no one's thinking about that once they start going door to door, mixing it up, deciding who's the best that day out there on the racetrack.

Look at that new Ford Focus Midget Series. Every car runs the same engine – one from an economy car, no less. But when the northeast Focus series opened at Seekonk in June it was the closest Midget racing anyone had seen in years. Those kids were *sick!*

Want a better example? What's the biggest racing series in the world? Right, it's NASCAR's Nextel Cup series. In Nextel Cup you can't tell one car from the other – even with a template. A Chevy is pretty much a Ford is pretty much a Dodge. But when they go racing nobody seems to care.

That's how it should be. The beauty of racing is the idea of a group of racers going at it toe to toe to see who's the fastest on that day. It's not supposed to be about the cars. You could have robots drive them, if that's the case. It's supposed to be about the racing.

WHAT'S UP WITH RACING

From Shorttrack Magazine, *2005*

T hings have gotten out of hand.
It used to be that you built a racecar following a few rules and then showed up with your creation to do battle against a bunch of guys who had done the same. It was fair way to compete on the racetrack.

No more. Nowadays you don't get your rules from one place, you get your engine. You get your shocks. In some series you get your *car!* Did you see that new Ford Focus Midgets Series? Imagine taking midgets, where you used to be welcome with some unique new engine, and making them all run power from an economy car. Yeah, sure, some rich team-owners won because they bought exotic big-buck power, but that only fueled the vision of tinkerers like "Mazda" Pete Pernisiglio. No one calls Brit Andersen's dad "Focus" Glen Andersen.

That's why I love a series like ISMA. Half the fun with the supers is strolling through the pits seeing what guys like Brian Allegresso and Clyde Booth have cooked up over the winter. Not all these guys have cubic dollars to play with. And what if they do? It's a free country. Do you prefer the Focus cars running in lockstep around Seekonk as if Bob Fosse choreographed the entire race, or NEMA, where they produced another wild race, some guys fast one place, some guys fast another, even if Ben Seitz won going away. Hey, so did Andersen, with power identical to the guys he smoked.

Want a better example? What's the biggest racing series in the world? Right, it's Formula One. Are they all running crate engines? Hardly. Practically every team has its own engine supplier – and they're not all small-block Chevies. Maybe they don't always run nose to tail, but an F-1 car is such an incredible technological marvel that when they fly by nobody seems to care.

That's how it should be. The beauty of racing is the idea of a group of builders going toe to toe to see who's the fastest on that day. It's not supposed to be about the drivers. Guys can run down the track if that's the case. It's supposed to be about the cars.

THE BUSINESS OF THE SPORT

From Shorttrack, 2006. *The bigger question is,"Is every sport a business?"*

I can't tell you how many times I've been cornered into answering the question, "Is racing really a sport?"

Usually the question dribbles out of the mouth of know-it-all sports reporters who give you all sorts of reasons why it isn't, all of them demonstrating a monumental ignorance of racing while betraying the real rationale for their belief; "I don't like racing."

Oh – and, "They don't serve enough buffets."

I'm not here to argue the point again, because, A; you know it is, and, B; you don't care. What I'm more concerned about is a question that fans of all sports are asking themselves more and more: "Is this a sport – or a business?"

Recently, Bill Ryan at Oxford Plains Speedway announced he was dropping pro stocks at his racetrack, and that ACT will rule his legendary Oxford 250. Oh, excuse me. His "*Banknorth* Oxford 250." I won't go into the reasons here that Ryan gave for doing it, other than to say they made perfect business-sense. Racetracks across New England have jettisoned their pro stock divisions, from Maine to Connecticut. And yes, you can't escape the fact that shorttracks are businesses, and they ignore that at their peril.

I'm even inclined to argue that such a business-decision can be made for sporting reasons, if, say, it's hard to put together a field of pro stocks decent enough to challenge pro stock racers or entertain crowds. But in the case of Oxford, that argument carries a great deal more weight when applied to weekly racing than when applied to the 250. Oh, excuse me again. The "Banknorth Oxford 250." I'm not aware of problems either with car-counts or competition at that event. Who would want to mess with that?

(Allow me to digress. I have no problem with businesses that support racing. I always try to mention sponsor-names of races and series. But I've developed an attitude about how far it's gone. Nextel has every right, to pick on just one marketing partner, to buy the name of NASCAR's most famous racing series, but they don't have a right to buy its history. Dale Eamhardt never won a NEXTEL Cup championship in his life. Now back to our regularly scheduled opinion.)

This, by the way, is not a knock on ACT. They are in the business of putting on great racing shows, and ACT's Tom Curley seems to have a knack for making great business-decisions that make great sport as well. But part of the 250's allure was that it featured the fastest late models in New England. Maine pro stocks, after all, are the state of the art around here. Sometimes it seems guys in Maine are nuts to spend the money they do. Isn't it great? Our investment is little more than the price of a ticket to see these guys go after each other in them.

So time will tell if Ryan's is a great sporting decision or not. Another by-the-way point, too. Don't confuse "business" with "money." George Steinbrenner never has. Apply the analogy closer to home and consider Jeremy Jacobs. He's been making a fine profit as owner of the Boston Bruins as his hockey team slid below mediocrity. His decision to clean house, hiring new coaches and management and signing for mega-bucks the best defenseman in the sport, was probably driven more by his friends busting him at parties than by any bottom line.

The 10,000 dollars Viveiros Insurance put up for the winner of the "Modified Madness" race at Seekonk Speedway in July likely will never be recouped in premiums. I don't think Joe Viveiros cared. What he got for his ten grand was True-Value top-gun Kirk Alexander and NASCAR Whelen Series star Ted Christopher getting together dramatically on the way to an Alexander victory.

Whelen regulars who raced that night will tell you of grief they got from NASCAR later. Well, it's NASCAR's own fault that its drivers chose to race in a race that was, after all, an open, non-points show If they cared about the *sport* of racing, they'd make it easier for tracks like Seekonk to host a Whelen race, and they'd make sure there were enough races to satiate the healthy appetites of modified racers, who choose to race mods for no business-reason I can see.

Oh, and one more thing. If they really cared about the sport, they wouldn't have passed up the chance to have a green-white-checkered finish in the modified race at NHIS in July just because they wanted to get the Busch TV show started on time.

But hey, that's business.

MORE STUFF

LIFE GOES ON ALL WINTER

From Trackside Magazine, *2002. The guys I covered had lives.*

The demands of racing can be all-consuming. No racer serious about winning can compromise time, money, attention or commitment. Slack off in any of these areas and your competitors will be happy to take up the slack in their obsession with surpassing you.

And forget about ``seasons.'' This effort now must continue 365 days each year. Most race teams are well into building their cars for next season even before the banquet celebrating their most recent successes. There is no time for resting on laurels for anyone who isn't retiring. Racing now is all about pressing on, doing more, doing better.

You might wonder if this isn't a perfect recipe for disaster. To be at their best racers must be passionate about their racing. Obviously they must love what they're doing to be this consumed by it. But isn't it true that ``Familiarity breeds contempt?'' Do anything 24/7 and don't you risk growing to hate it? Certainly you risk squeezing the joy out of it. Doesn't another saying go ``Absence makes the heart grow fonder?''

Not every seasoned and successful racer would admit it, but evidence suggests many of them believe that axiom anyway. While they don't forget about racing, when it gets cold and northern racetracks close their gates for the winter they turn to other activities

143

to stir their competitive juices. Or, even if they don't necessarily subscribe to the aforemenioned theory, concessions to other responsibilities in their lives still can divert their attention away from their primary obsession.

Regardless, here's one writer who would subscribe to the theory that, whatever a driver's motivation for seeking diversion, there nonetheless is evidence that diversions certainly contribute to making racers the interesting people they invariably are. Show me one overly obsessed athlete and I'll see one boring individual indeed.

No one could ever accuse Dave Dion of being boring. No one can accuse him of underachieving, either. For years the Dion race team has been doing more than most NASCAR Busch North teams have done with far fewer resources at its disposal.

Certainly the team's head honcho, Roger Dion, has worked hard with relentless focus to get the most out of the resources available to the family-business of stockcar racing. But Dave, one of the most successful drivers ever to turn a wheel on a New England oval, has been less obsessed.

``For me,'' admits Dion, ``racing is secondary to living. Racing is no longer the primary part of my life. It hasn't been for maybe the last ten years.''

So how much does this veteran scale back his attention to racing when winter rears its blustery head?

``I don't do anything racing in the winter,'' Dion declares, ``absolutely nothing.''

What? Nothing? Doesn't that drive him crazy? Well – no.

``I much prefer the off-season to the racing season. I get to spend a lot of time with my grandchildren. I got some snowmobiles; we ride them a lot. I do a lot of reading. I love tech manuals.

``Christmas is a big deal. All the winter holidays are a big deal, because summer holidays don't exist for me. Even Halloween – I take my grandchildren out.''

Dion is a particularly happy camper these days. With the New England Patriots' unlikely and exciting championship he's found a reason for a celebration like he hasn't experienced in years. Why, you probably can compare it to when he won his last championship, in

NASCAR's Busch North series in 1996. But only if you want to damn the Pats' Super Bowl win with faint praise.

``Football is my first love," declares Dion. ``I love (it) more than racing. Those guys are my heroes."

Now Dave Dion is a throwback to another era, the era of true sportsmen. Even he would admit that his time has almost passed; ``I guess I'm like a retired racer who's still racing," he says.

Look instead to Mike Olson. He's part of the new breed of racer, totally focused on his chosen sport, a man with no time for frivolities such as being a fan of some stick-and-ball sport.

``I'm definitely a 365-days-a-year racer," he agrees.

There we are. No time for any playing around for Mike Olson – right?

``Well, I do play some indoor soccer," he admits, ``And I try to play some basketball."

So worry instead about the obsessions of Rick Martin. They have compelled him to titles at Seekonk Speedway as well as Thompson. Even in the dead of winter you'll find him in his race shop, preparing cars to compete – at Big Boys Toys in the Silver City Galleria mall in Taunton, Mass.

The cars he's working on these days are radio-control versions of stock cars, and they'll fit into a good-size toolbox. They're the perfect little diversion to the demands of racing the big cars, just a little light entertainment on a winter evening. A nice way to relax in the off-season, right Rick?

``Actually I'm working harder now than I did in the summer," says Martin with a laugh of incredulity. ``(I'm racing against) sponsored guys there that race nationally.

``I won two weeks in a row but then I've gotten a second and a third. I've got to start working harder."

That hardly sounds like a diversion from racing. For that look to ISMA Supermodified and Thompson pro stock driver Chris Perley. He's involved in an activity far removed from racing. But he's not motivated by a need to keep himself occupied to fill an overabundance of time on his hands. Quite the opposite, in fact.

``You have to do everything you put off all summer," he explains.

``Like I'm putting a deck on my house right now – in the middle of winter – because I'll never get it done in the summer. I'll never get to use it, but my wife will enjoy it.''

As with Dion, Perley is trying to make up for the loss of important opportunities.

``I try to be around the house a little more,'' he explains, ``and be the `family man.' ''

Argue if you will whether any of these racers is better for having gotten away from the sport for a while. But consider an old story from my days sucking dust as a motocrosser. Years ago the best motocross racers in the country came from one of two areas. One of them, obviously enough, was California. The other was New England, where the sport actually was born in America.

Somebody decided it would be interesting to pit the best of the West versus the best from New England in a head-to-head showdown, but a lot of folks felt it would be no contest. The Californians, you see, got to ride year-round, graced as they were by temperate weather throughout the year. The New Englanders, meanwhile, parked their bikes in November and didn't fire them up again until March. The break represented four or five months when the California hotshoes were out gaining an edge on the East Coasters. The edge, many felt, would be particularly evident right out of the starting gate as the well-tuned Westerners blew the cobwebs out of the rusty boys from back East.

I'd like to tell you that the New England contingent blew the doors off the Californians. It was a more even match than that. In fact, Team California ultimately took the title. But it was close, and, if anything, the Easterners started out of the gate with the edge before their opponents realized they'd gotten it all wrong. While they looked at the early races as just the next set of motos, the guys from New England were absolutely pumped to be racing again after a winter of hanging out in their garages. Absence had made their hearts – and their bikes – go faster.

You're wise enough to realize they'll be no flies on any of the guys mentioned here come spring.

HIGH CLASS

From Shorttrack Magazine, 1996.

Contrast has a way of making things clearer. Seeing the opposite ends of the spectrum can illuminate both extremes. Put another way, you won't know just how slow your Geo is until you drive a Vette.

I've always thought I liked Tony Stewart. Surely he was mouthy and self-absorbed, but amidst a world of Stepford wives always making nice with each other, always appreciating everything and everyone, always loving every track, and always driving a "great car my team gave me today," even after sliding into the wall while struggling in 23rd, Tony Stewart's candor seemed a continual breath of fresh air in a very stuffy and pretentious business.

I thought it was cool when it was announced he'd be driving a modified in the Whelen Series race at New Hampshire in July. Not that I thought Stewart was going to show the Whelen Modified drivers the fast way around the Magic Mile. Life isn't that simple, and mod drivers aren't that impressed. No, I figured he'd go fast and acquit himself well and that one of the series-regulars would come home escorted by a mass of competition, just as always happens when the mods play at New Hampshire. If he was lucky, I figured Stewart would be a top-five finisher, might even be in that lead pack.

Tony Stewart ran hard at New Hampshire. He qualified decently, headed for the front of the field and toyed with the lead before contact sent him to the pits and a scramble to finish a solid ninth.

I figured he'd had a couple of hours of fun and now could return to earning his living defending a NEXTEL Cup title at one of the series's toughest tracks. I beat feet to Star Speedway, looking forward to an evening there.

A day later I'm reading the newspaper. I learn that the contact that sent Stewart to the pits came at the hands of Jerry Marquis. I also learned Stewart was seething over it after the race.

"You come down to race in these races and if you do better than these guys they resent it," Stewart complained. He went on about how he "used to respect" Marquis until Marquis evidently put him out because he was so jealous of Stewart.

All this was vintage Stewart, easy enough to laugh off under normal circumstances. But I was having a harder time laughing it off after an evening at Star. I thought about an incident that happened at Star on the cool-down lap after the Super Street heat. As the cars rolled down the backstretch, defending division-champion Ron Bolduc had turned down into the side of Tony Carroll's car. Intent had been obvious. I was a bit stunned.

A Bolduc crewmember sitting nearby told me, "This has been brewing for a couple of weeks."

I went looking for Bolduc, a normally soft-spoken bear of a guy I'd talked to plenty of times, including for a feature in the charter issue of Shorttrack. I found him walking away from the Dave Lind Tires truck.

"In all my years racing," he said to me, "I've never lost my cool like that."

The whole affair had started with incidents on the racetrack between Carroll and him. Of course.

"He told my car owner he was going to wreck the car. Then when he ran into me after the checkered flag I said 'You want to play that game? I can play that game, too.' "

The problem was Carroll's contact had been unintentional.

"His girlfriend told me I cut his tire. I just went over to the tire-truck and told them to give him a new tire, and I'll pay for it."

Bolduc spotted Carroll over my shoulder, heading toward where

Bolduc's car was parked.

"I have to go talk to him," he said.

So a day later I'm reading the sports page, thinking about Bolduc going out of his way to right a wrong he felt he'd committed, embarrassed about the one time he lost it on the racetrack. I thought about Stewart, saying he'd "lost respect" for Jerry Marquis, and how he'd "come down" to drive the faster, better-handling, closer-racing modifieds. And I thought about the idea that Jerry Marquis would be jealous of Tony Stewart a day after his third-place finish in the Busch East race, and his finish in the mod race one place better than Stewart, and whether Stewart's finish even mattered to him at all, since the mods were where Marquis was earning his own living.

And I decided that, as fast as Stewart is, when it came to class that Saturday he'd been a Geo in a field of Vettes.

KRAFTING A PLAN

From the Attleboro Sun Chronicle, *1997. Don't think the racetrack ever did get built in Foxboro. They* did *build a mall. And Seekonk stepped up its act.*

It's been fun watching Robert Kraft try to find a way to build a shining new venue for the shining new version of the old neighborhood-football team.

Kraft has been telling anyone who'd listen that he needs our money to build a stadium for his New England Patriots, and more money than just the cash we put down to watch the Pats play.

He's made this plea before. both. in the Bay State and in Rhode Island. But when public officials have asked the question of what's in it for the rest of us, Kraft has struggled to come up wtth a good enough answer.

Now, though, Bob Kraft has sweetened the pot. Good for him; that's how negotiating is supposed to work. I mean, whom does he think he's dealing with, somebunch a rubes in Baltimore?

Normally this column would not be the place to read aoout this particular news-story. But Kraft has gotten racefans into the debate with one particular aspect of his latest proposal. We wonder if that was a good idea.

You may have read what some have had to say about the idea of a

"NASCAR track" being built in the vicinity of Foxboro Stadium as part of a "sports-related entertainment-complex."

The objections raised by the more ignorant among them haven't gotten beyond uninformed concerns about noise. As if 60,000 screaming maniacs on a Monday night won't keep you up.

More informed commentators have offered their doubts about what chance a new track in this region would have of landing a coveted Winston Cup date.

Without question there's not much chance of that, and not because New England fans wouldn't pack the place. They have at New Hampshire Speedway two times this year.

The problem here is that there are few plaees in this country where fans wouldn't do the same and too many places where they don't have the chance.

But is that what the Kraft Proposal means when it refers to a "NASCAR track?" Are they focused on getting a Winston Cup date?

There are other series that a NASCAR track could host, including Busches north and south, modifieds and Craftsman trucks. Dates in those series likely would be more available.

Some New England track-owners would just as soon give up the Busch North and Featherlite Modified races they already have. With the Busch series, especially, the complications of hosting a race can tax the resources of a neighborhood shorttrack.

But a NASCAR track doesn't have to have any tour races at all. Monadnock, N.H., Speedway runs only weekly races for local drivers and crowns its own Winston Series champion every year.

Southeastern Massachusetts could use an operation on that level. The only shorttrack in the area is a crusty old place with a management team that refuses to remove its collective head from a deep ditch of greasy sand.

Indeed most drivers at Seekonk Speedway rightly or wrongly consider the place their only alternative if they want to keep racing on a weekly basis. They'd travel elsewhere in a heartbeat.

But the question for the Krafts should be whether their proposal has any focus at all.

Beyond that, it's curious to bring up building a racetrack during the debate over the wisdom and necessity of procuring public funds to support a private enterprise.

The last guy to build a big-league stadium in New England was Bob Bahre when he built New Hampshire Speedway.

Bahre didn't go looking for public money to build his racetrack. He dug the money out of his own pocket.

In fact, when the town of Loudon questioned its ability to provide the level of services a new racetrack in its midst ultimately would demand, Bahre dug even deeper and contributed to the financing of the public services his new track would require of the area.

Bet you didn't know that, did you, Bob?

A PLEA FOR SUPERS

From Shorttrack Magazine, *2005. Supers haven't been at Seekonk in a while.*

An open letter to Seekonk Speedway:

Hi folks! Boy, it's great that Opening Day finally arrives Saturday. But I've got to tell you, something is missing this year.

Now, I don't mean to be a pain, even though you're pretty used to writers such as me being precisely that. So let me make a few points here.

I grew up in Seekonk. Seekonk Speedway was the first racetrack I ever went to. I consider it "home." Even after years of traveling around the region and seeing races everywhere from Pennsylvania to Maine I still haven't been anywhere with better racing. Seekonk's fields always are full, your divisions always have more than enough high-quality equipment and talented drivers, and the racing is as competitive as any anywhere.

Just last week I found myself – for the scaty-eighth time – declaring to someone who'd never seen a race at Seekonk that I could almost guarantee any time he went he would see at least one feature-race come down to the wire.

Furthermore, there is no better place in the world to see maybe my favorite form of racecar, a midget, do its thing. Indeed, if I were trying to explain the appeal of racing to some person who was asking me how I could stand watching a bunch of cars go around in circles, I'd take them to a midget event at Seekonk. That person might not come away a diehard fan for life, but the heart-stoppingly obvious point would be made that racing wasn't simply driving around.

In short, I love Seekonk, and I thank my lucky stars every year when the gates swing open there for another season.

Okay, then. Enough sucking up. It's time to get to the point.

How in the name of Bentley Warren could you let the supermods get away?

Supers, for those of you who haven't had the pleasure, are the most powerful racecars to ever turn wheels on a shorttrack. A super weighs little more than many behemoth motorcycles yet has more power than a NEXTEL Cup car. A super on a shorttrack is so fast it bends time. A super simply is the ultimate extreme of sport's most extreme spectacle.

And supers at Seekonk are a couple of steps beyond that extreme. I would suggest, as a matter of fact, that they would actually qualify as one of those experiences not to be missed by any true fan of racing, in the manner that a baseball fan from Missouri just knows that Fenway Park must be visited at least once in a lifetime. Supers at Seekonk represent, then, a pilgrimage for a true racing fan.

You probably didn't even realize the magnitude of the "Supers at Seekonk"experience, running around trying to get your shows off. I, on the other hand, was basking in the glow of it. Let me share a bit with you.

First off, Seekonk's clean and convenient pits are perfect for poking around in the midst of these magnificent beasts. There seemingly are no two supers alike. Motorheads can entertain themselves just checking out the cars.

But it is on the track where the experience turns mystical. Seekonk, of course, is a handling track to begin with, and a super sticks more rubber to the road than half a field of pro stocks. The biggest wings in racing push them into the asphalt even further.

Some small tracks just can't contain all the fury wrought by a pack of supers. Many drivers suspected that might be the case at Seekonk.

They were wrong.

"I really worried we wouldn't be able to put on much of a show when I first saw the track," admitted two-time International Supermodified Association champion Chris Perley last week, "but I couldn't believe the place, once I went out there."

Neither could a lot of fans. If you're looking for a word to describe watching supers at your track, "frightening" would work. The supers at Seekonk came out of the corners and threw off a wave of hot air, moisture and spent-rubber in their wake. Fans close to the wall were seen scampering to higher seats, their faces, half grinning, half grimacing, turned away from the onslaught. And it seemed that before the last morsels of rubber had bounced off their faces the supers were flying by again.

The drivers were in their glory, and none more than some of the low-dollar guys who usually are hopelessly over-matched against the series's top teams. Rick Wentworth will tell you. He races ISMA with one cast-off engine and a car he copied from Vic Miller, Perley's boss. At Seekonk last year he drove brilliantly to his first ISMA victory. This was great stuff, and anyone who knew anything understood the significance of it. Like me, they loved it and couldn't wait for more.

And now? And now, you open the season with your weekly divisions, and without ISMA to kick things off with the sort of explosion a season-opener should enjoy. The competitors from ISMA are perplexed. Why, Seekonk was on the 2006 schedule at one point. Then it just slipped away.

Well. I'm here to tell you, they'd come back in a heartbeat. What'll it take, Seekonk? You must have a few bucks lying around now that you've cancelled your NASCAR sanction and won't have to wheelbarrow bushels of cash down to Daytona so they can put together more marketing deals for women's shoes. Bring the magic back, please.

THE BULLRING
GRADUATE RACING PROGRAM

From Trackside Magazine, *2003. This might work, but you'd likely have to start from scratch. Still...*

Everyone has their megalomaniacal fantasies. So do I, although in my advancing years I've settled for creating ever-smaller worlds.

One world to which my mind occasionally travels is a world where I rule a weekly racetrack. There I would avoid every error ever committed by every promoter and introduce many innovations that would be hailed as revolutionary.

I've little interest in actually inhabiting this world, mind you. There should be no illusions about the difficulty of running a racetrack successfully. That I could find something to criticize at any track I visit has far more to do with my propensity for cynicism than it does with a poor effort on the part of the folks who might run it. Besides, if you read the last part of this column you'll realize, if you don't already, that I am in no position to direct criticism at anybody else.

But I got to rolling an idea around in my increasingly addled brain recently while considering the adoption of crate engines at race tracks across the country. Crate engines have enjoyed acceptance at many tracks in the last couple of years. Lee of course now requires them in its late models. Seekonk has introduced them as an option in both its Pro Stock and Sportsman divisions. Monadnock has done it with its pro stocks. I'm missing some examples, but you get the picture.

This is a positive trend. Eight-cylinder engines were in danger of extinction, although the SUVs running around making life dangerous for fools in Metros (help!) offer fodder for future engine builders.

I don't want to see the livelihoods of many talented builders threatened, but it's always seemed there were not enough talented builders to service top divisions at most tracks. And face it; expenses for engine-building and maintenance have grown out of proportion to all potential for reward.

On the other hand, there is a selection of crate engines just from GM that could provide controlled power over a range of divisions. We've all heard of GM's ZZ-4 engines. My particular fantasy would include the ZZ-4 at the top of the food chain. This is an idea that I believe would facilitate advancement and growth at my racetrrack. Its essential element is that a track could present three divisions with only two choices of engine and chassis. A driver could build a typical street stock based on a metric chassis. A crate engine would be specified, as would a rearend and a fairly narrow racing tire. At the other extreme would be a pro stock, with typical chassis rules, ten-inch tires and quick-change rears. In this division the ZZ-4 would be required.

Do you know where I'm going (or do you wish I'd just go away?)? The division between the two would allow the pro stock chassis with the streeter engine and drivetrain, right down to the tires. Street stock teams could move up to the middle division (Let's call them ``Super Stocks") simply by acquiring a pro stock chassis. They'd already have the engines, rears and tires. This would allow them to make the change gradually. Perhaps they could try out an end-of-season big show. Or do both divisions over the course of a season. They'd be learning about setting up their super stocks knowing they're preparing for future advancement. In a few seasons they can take the same get-your-feet-wet move up to the pro stocks.

The market for used equipment also would open up significantly if, say, super stock teams could sell engines, rearends, and even wheels and tires to new teams getting into the sport.

Hey, it's just an idea, flawed I'm sure. But after all, it is my track.

NASCAR HEAT ?

From Shortrack Magazine, 2006. You already know I find Cup races boring.

Writing columns is a gas. There are none of the responsibilities of reporting. Columnists don't have to worry about getting both sides of a story; heck, they don't even have to be newsworthy!

Believe it or not (if you know me), it took a while before this point got pounded into my head. I've worked with a few editors over the years, and I've always concerned myself with giving them material that served their needs. Yet almost always editors would respond to voiced concerns with "It's your column. Write about whatever you want."

Still, it was some time before I actually indulged myself in sharing my racing fantasies with readers (No, not the "He wins the Daytona 500 – in a '52 Studebaker!" one. I save that for bouts of childish self-indulgence). Gradually, though, I began to share my fantasies of racecars, divisions, or other utopian musings, items that, whatever their impracticalities, provided food for thought if nothing else. And here I am, writing right at the front of *Shorttrack*, without even an editor to answer to. Who's going to stop me now?

Bear with me. I often complain about NASCAR's NEXTEL Cup Series. Yeah, I know, this is *Shorttrack*, and we cover New England, but again, bear with me, because I have an idea that would make just about the coolest NEXTEL Cup race ever held.

I'm like you. I hate time-trials. Save for the Indy 500, they bore me. I suppose they make sense if you're deciding the starting field for a 300-mile race, but you know what? I'm not so wild about 300-mile races, either.

I will enthusiastically endorse the idea that NEXTEL Cup racing brings together the best racers in America. Yet NASCAR makes every race a race of perseverance, a race of attrition and a race of concentration before a few teams who find themselves at the front of the field with ten laps to go possibly get to make it a race of – well – a race.

I can go to just about any shorttrack that gets this magazine and know that I'm going to see a thrilling race-finish. I might even see five of them, and they'll come over a few hundred laps of real racing. And every time I do, the thought will at least drift by my brain that it'd be mighty cool if once – just once – NASCAR got together its NEXTEL Cup competitors at some shorttrack for an old-fashioned weekly-series style event.

Forget chases to the championship. Wouldn't you like to see a pack of Cup points-leaders going at it over only 15 or 20 laps to earn the right just to make the points-paying show? Wouldn't you like to see Kurt Busch start from the back of that field? Can you imagine the show Tony Stewart would put on trying to advance from a consi? How about Jeff Gordon and Dale, Jr., fighting for the last transfer spot?

Do you think this sort of stuff might get the attention of all those folks who complain that a Cup race is just bunch of people driving in a circle for hour after hour?

Goodness, I salivate at the thought of it. Think about where they might run such a race. Bristol. That was easy.

Of course, I have a better chance of winning Indy in a Studie Starlight Coupe than of seeing such a race. Cup teams never would go for this. All that money they spend would be wasted if they never made the feature. It might cut down on sponsors' precious "exposure-time." It certainly would be too great a risk for these highly-financed professional operations.

Balderdash, of course. The equipment any local pro stock team brings to the track every week is no less dear to them than the multi-million dollar cars are to the multi-billion dollar teams. The passion is no cooler. Packing up early hurts everyone who's ever done it as their race circled the track without them.

Still, you know this is fantasy.

It's probably just as well. NASCAR already is devouring too much of itself, running Cup races from Richmond opposite NASCAR Weekly-Series events going on around the country. We don't have to educate racefans too lazy to walk beyond the beer in the fridge that there's a better way to do it. Let them come out to the track, like we do, and support those guys so passionate about their pro stocks.

CHARACTERS

THE ASTLES ARE RACERS

*From Trackside Magazine, 1999. One of my favorite stories –
because of the experience.*

In the world of commerce that racing has become everything must be
taken seriously. There's no room for messing around. You must seek
success with everything you do. And the proper image must be
maintained to insure that appropriate support is provided as you search
for that success.

Seriousness is a fact of life in every pursuit in society today, of
course. People devote more energy to trying to create a perfect leisure
experience than they spend simply having a good time. On the other
hand, is there anyone anywhere who is ``simply having a good time,"
anyway?

Are there any racers? You might wonder as you view the young driver
who's won his first race in some bigtime, dream-destination of a race
series. After his calm, almost bored responses to a few interview
questions, undoubtedly with mention of every sponsor who bought
add-space on his racecar, you may ask yourself why the driver even
bothered taking the green flag.

This driver may live on to forge a successful racing career, but will he be left with any tales to tell his grandchildren?

Odds are that few drivers of today will be able to match stories with the likes of the Astle brothers. The years of racing by these five southern-New England drivers produced victories that equal success by any measure. But the stories they tell and those that are told of them provide a view of a raucous experience filled with a joy lost to the serious business of modern racing.

On a recent summer evening, Dan, Deke and Jon Astle drew some lawn chairs together in the yard behind the house of their brother Fred, who'd passed away in January. Absent as well was Bobby, who'd be left at the mercy of his brothers' memories. Joining his uncles was Fred Jr., in the midst of a stellar season at the family's old stomping grounds, Seekonk Speedway.

They'd gathered to share their memories with a writer who lived a deprived childhood, cursed to grow up in a family that wasn't much interested in stock car racing. By the time the writer got a license and began making regular visits to the self-proclaimed ``Action Track of the East," the action for the elder Astles already was winding down.

The careers of the Astles spanned a period from the early 1950s, when Fred traded a '34 Ford for his first racecar, to the late 1970s, when Jon finally parked his last one.

``Our father thought racing was too dangerous," remembered Jon of Fred's first season. ``He didn't want him out there. So he made him get rid of (the car)."

``When he got rid of that car," added Deke, ``he built a new car over the winter. He did pretty good with that. It was a good car."

Evidently, then, despite their father's initial objections, a racing family had been born. So, too, began a saga of, well, just call them misadventures. Witness Dan's introduction to racing shortly after Fred's.

``That's probably when they first started the Bombers," he recalled. ``(They allowed) anything but a Ford.

``I knew they wouldn't let me race one night because I was too young."

One of his brothers was happy to solve that problem. Which one it was no longer held importance and so was left open to question.

164

``We all got the same handwriting anyway,'' Jon pointed out.

Soon the other brothers would follow Fred and Dan into racecars. Each's involvement started as a hand given in one of the garages behind the Astle home. Soon a new car would come together. Consider Deke's effort on behalf of Jon as typical of how it happened.

``He built me my first car,'' Jon explained. ``We cut all the pipes up and we told the welder to get to the track early. He charged us five dollars to weld the pipes in. I went out and won the feature.''

Jon continued winning in his Bomber-class racecar. Finally, Lou Guiliano, who was running Seekonk Speedway at the time, issued a warning to Jon.

`` `You win one more time,' '' Jon related. `` `We're sending you to the A-Class.'

``Me and George Martin – we both wore red shirts. I won again, so I drove right into the pits. We had it all set up. I got out and we acted like he'd driven.

``They caught us,'' Jon conceded with a smile.

While it was great of Deke to help his brother out, Jon certainly earned the hand. Brother acts are notorious for their volatility, and the passionate Astles were a great example of the theory.

``I was outside helping Fred,'' said Jon. ``He's got me racing around. `Go get this. Go do that.' He went in the garage. I took off for the house. Here comes a four-way lug wrench.''

Fortunately Fred's pitch of a lug wrench was a little short on distance even if he had the range. The lug wrench rolled socket-over-socket down the yard to catch Jon in the back of the legs. The point was made, and Jon lived to learn it.

Although Dan's racing came early in the family's experience and Bobby's came late, there was plenty of brother-against-brother action.

``Me, Deke and Fred ran quite a bit together,'' said Jon.

``Everybody said we always set up so nobody could pass us,'' added Deke. ``We raced each other harder that anybody!''

Like the time Seekonk Speedway's legendary Anthony Venditti promoted a race at the old Bryar Motorsport Park, the racetrack that preceeded New Hampshire International Speedway in Loudon. Jon won the race on the road course's crude tri-oval section.

``He cheated that day,'' remarked Deke.

``I did not,'' Jon replied.

``It was as hot as hell that day,'' Deke explained. ``The rule was you couldn't take your hood off.''

``I asked,'' argued Jon, ``and they said `go ahead.' You were in a hurry to go out. I waited to go out. You guys had the old brakes. I had the Buick brakes – the finned brakes.''

``It wasn't the brakes,'' concluded Deke with a smirk. ``It was the heat.''

This hardly was the only time the Astles traveled away from their home track. They ran at long-gone places like Norwood and Westboro, at still-running tracks like Star and Waterford. They ran dirt, out at Lebanon and back at Lakeville, where Deke won 17 races in a row.

They raced at Thompson more than once, heading out there often with the veteran Johnny Tripp. Deke recalled the fun they had with Tripp when they traveled together.

``We'd say, `The last one to the car drives,' and we'd all pile in the car. He'd always be the last one to the car and the driver's seat would be empty.

``We'd get on him the whole way back – `Pass 'em John! Pass 'em! We'll pay the fines.' One time he finally told us to just be quiet. So he goes driving into Chepachet (RI) and we ain't saying anything. And that's when a cop pulls him over.

``He had to go to court,'' laughed Deke. ``It turns out the fine is something like ten bucks. And the court costs are 14 bucks. We said, `Hey John, we said we'd pay the fine.' ''

The Astle legend was forged, however, at the legend-builder of racetracks, Seekonk. It included hard driving, crude but effective home-built race cars, and one other point that was revealed by one interjected comment in the course of the evening.

``There was one rule they came up with...'' Jon began.

``That we always had to get around,'' Deke interrupted, laughing.

The comment came up as the subject of Deke's Crosley race car was discussed. The car was not one of the nascent Mini-Stock Crosleys that comprised one of Venditti's brainstorm-creations. It was a gorgeous little car with a 327 Chevy that was cobbled together to

166

beat another of Venditti brainstorm-rules. But it was all on the level, protested Deke.

``Me and Earl Grant and Venditti – we all went to a restaurant across the street from the track,'' he explained. ``We drew it up on a napkin. He said, `That's okay. As long as you weld the springs up to Crosley frame-rails.' ''

Which of course ended up being the only function the Crosley frame-rails served. No matter. However neat the car may have looked, it didn't get the job done.

``When it got sideways,'' Deke admitted, ``it spun like one of those midgets.''

As the years passed there grew less and less opportunity for such creativity. By the time Vega and Pinto-bodied modifieds were the rule at Seekonk, they became the rides of choice for the Astles as well. Still the independence of the Astles revealed itself in other ways. For one thing they continued to prove their mettle in low-buck creations even as the competition grew more expensive, and professional builders began to take over that component of racing. And it's hard to believe that any Troyer-built creation ever took the track at Seekonk with a ten-year old kid riding its transmission tunnel.

``I loved it,'' declared Fred Jr., of his first experience at speed in a racecar. Yes – at speed.

``Fred sat him on the driveshaft,'' said Deke, ``and went out full-bore.''

Five years later, the fire fanned with mini-bikes and karts, Fred Jr. debuted in a '68 Camaro built to Seekonk's Charger specs. His father continued building cars for him, including a Charlie Rose-chassised pro stock in the late '80s. That car still sits in one of the garages behind Fred's house.

``That's pretty much the last car he built,'' said Fred Jr.

Fred built another car during the same period. It sits in the same garage. It's a '41 Ford coupe with a flathead V-8, built to replicate one of his favorite racecars.

``Look at that thing,'' Fred Jr., directed. ``Look inside. Look at the floorboards. The car was in beautiful shape. Why he ever cut it up...

``But he was determined to build this car.''

Fred maintained that determination to the end of his life. Days before he died he could be found on staging, painting his house.

``You couldn't stop him," said his son as he stood with his uncles outside another of the garages at his father's house, now his own.

``He had an oxygen hose running out the window to where he was working," recalled Deke.

Fred Jr., the last of the Astles still racing competitively, surveyed the scene in the gathering darkness. White light spilled out of two open garages. Racecars, in various stages of construction, peeked out from behind the open doors. A group of people, racing people, milled around at the edge of the light, content to bask in the reflected glow of unforgettable memories.

``It's been a long time since we've had a night like this," Fred Jr., realized out loud, ``a long time since there's been a bunch of people around.

``It hasn't happened since my father died."

One can only hope that nights like this don't disappear with the racers who raced before it was a business.

THE ASTLES, PART II: BROTHERS IN SPIRIT

From Trackside Magazine, *1999. Yes, this ran before the previous piece, but they do work in this order.*

Racing's technology runs rampant, and those competitors who try to ignore it soon are run over by it. That's the truism, anyway, and who can deny it when the deepest pockets keep getting filled with the largest purses.

Even street stock investments seem to be getting out of hand. Never mind that you likely could have campaigned a Winston Cup car in the 1980s for what it costs to run competitively on NASCAR's Featherlite Modified Tour today.

And can you remember when modifieds really were just that – street car bits and pieces modified for use on the Northeast's shorttracks? Can you remember the guys who built these hulking machines in their garages? Do you know grizzled racefans who insist that racing hasn't been the same since car builders started to forsake the anvil for the parts catalog?

I started giving this some thought after visiting the home of New England racing legend Fred Astle for a piece on the Astle brothers that will appear in an upcoming issue of *Trackside*. Astle's son, Fred Jr., was conducting a tour of his late father's garage, which exuded the comfortably-cluttered ambiance of an eccentric tinkerer's workshop.

In the back of the garage sat a naked roller Fred Sr. had built for his son to race at Seekonk Speedway. The car was classic Seekonk pro stock down to its Camaro front clip, as incorporated into the frame by another local legend, Charlie Rose. From there the senior Astle had taken over and produced a car that still sat ready to race, save for its outer skin.

``This is the last car my father built, really," Fred Jr. realized, before pointing out offhandedly, ``Of course, all this sheet metal came off of an old refrigerator or something."

Yow! Nobody would do that anymore, at least not on a pro stock. Or would they?

This second-generation racing Astle offered an intriguing answer to the question.

``I may race it as a sportsman (at Seekonk)," he offered, ``or set it up to run as a late model somewhere."

Could anyone still do that? Can you still race somewhere against computer-fabricated, Five Star-bodied, professionally-prepared racecars in a creation that ensconces you in old refrigerator doors?

Hell, even a decade ago when he built the car, Fred Astle, Sr., appreciated the irony of what he had wrought.

``The car used to have an instrument panel on it he cut from a stove," observed Astle, Jr. ``He even left the nameplate on it. It said 'Hotpoint' or something."

Astle's old pro stock left me wondering if maybe there are some still in racing who approached their cars with this healthy attitude. Maybe there are some car builders with enough confidence in their own judgement or enough contempt for our ``spend before you think" modern mentality to scavenge and scrounge where others would spend.

Bob Potter has every reason to be confident in his abilities on the track and off. He's successfully raced both the modifieds that were cobbled together out of junkyard parts and Troyer-built modern marvels. But his avoidance of the checkbook-racing theory has more to do with his checkbook than it does with his theories.

``We make everything we can build now so we can afford to race," Potter admitted in mid-September as he nursed a damaged rib suffered

170

in an SK at Stafford. He went on to recite a laundry list of components his team routinely fabricates.

``We make our own upper and lower A-arms. We make all our own struts. Spindles are a tough thing to make, but if we make them ourselves we can make two for the price of one.

``We decided if we wanted a new car we'd have to build it ourselves. So we made a jig off of our old car and then used it to make a new one.   And we make our own bodies; we have a big old hand-brake.

``It would be nice to make our own wheels but we don't have a jig to do that. Even in a good season we go through ten to twelve wheels.''

It's those high-ticket yet vulnerable parts that run the expense of racing way past anybody's projections from before the season starts. And usually it's labor that makes the parts expensive.

``We put a new tail on our car ourselves and it costs $100,'' explains Pete Fiandaca, another veteran with a reputation for doing things himself. ``You go to a shop and that guy's got to get 800 - 900 bucks to do it. I'm not blaming them, either. It's just the way it is.''

`That's because expertise required to fabricate pieces such as these does not come easy. For Fiandaca, Potter and their crews it came after decades of competition and scores of expensive lessons. Of course, that becomes its own advantage.

``You learn a lot more about the car,'' Potter states simply, proceeding to describe a trial-and-error process of hands-on education that's rare with some teams.

Fiandaca would agree with Potter on this point – and then some. Currently racing his own pro stock as well as a 350 super and lightning truck for others at Star Speedway, he believes some teams could stand a little more hands-on education.

``I don't know if there's a lot of guys who could even change tires,'' he declares, noting, ``You go to the races and there's a line of guys at the tire truck.''

However, he believes that the tracks have contributed to a lack of innovative car builders today.

``They don't have a division where you can be creative,'' he says. ``A guy comes in and he makes his car a little offset – something that doesn't cost nothing. And they write all kinds of rules to stop him. They should write rules against tires."

But teams don't have to employ draftsmen and welders to save time thumbing through catalogs and the expense of doing business with the companies that sell from them. Ronnie Pond has earned a reputation for campaigning cars that crudely express their interest in function over form at Seekonk Speedway. Currently he's working with Len Ellis, who turned the controls of his pro stock over to Dick Houlihan while he recovers from an injury. Pond's found another way to save money racing.

``We try to sell what's bent for stuff that's less bent," he declares only somewhat facetiously. He explains further.

``What happens is people see parts on someone else's car and they buy them and put them on their car and they don't know how to make them work. They're still competitive parts, but everyone's trying to keep up with the Joneses.

``It's more than having what everyone has. It's knowing why (something) works and how to make it work."

Pond has assembled his own warehouse of racing parts. His garage is full of slightly-used parts that didn't magically transform somebody's slow racecar into a fast one. He makes a habit of taking truckloads to swap meets and then returning home with truckloads of different parts, hopefully with about the same amount of money with which he left.

While Pond is every bit the fabricator that Potter and Fiandaca are, he's more of a scavenger. For example, while Potter bends his own bodies and Fiandaca starts with one store-bought one and repairs it until it's aluminum foil, Pond stick his nose into the proverbial discount bin at Rhino-Hide.

``I got a deal for the rejects," he says. ``I get them if they didn't come out of the mold right or if the gel-coat color was screwed up."

There is one aspect of the scavenger's trade that is gone forever.

``The only (street-car part) that's used on a pro stock is the mirror," laments Fiandaca. ``That's the only thing you can get out of a junkyard that'll work."

``I can't think of anything that still comes off a road car," agrees Potter.

172

``It was nice years ago." he remembers. ``You'd go to a junkyard. You'd get your whole steering set-up. I think one time we were using A-frames off of Lincolns. Now it's just over the counter."

Of course, not totally. There still are all those entry-level divisions, with their metric chassis and police-car motors. Don't think that doesn't hold some allure even for racers who supposedly moved on to bigger and better things years ago.

Pete Fiandaca, for one, is building a street stock right now.

WHEN I WAS YOUR AGE

From Trackside Magazine, 2002. *From the Memorial Day issue. Veterans remember when they were rookies.*

So here, in the midst of *Trackside's* annual Memorial Day retrospective, you find a column featuring racers still plying their trade at the dawn of the 21st century.

Racers these days, including at least a couple featured here, head into battle strapped to the seats of metal-flaked and airbrushed asphalt rocket ships. Car builders exploit astronomical levels of technology (not to mention invesment). Their cars are computer-designed and then tig-welded out of chrome-moly, to which sophisticated components are attached by unobtanium fasteners applied with a sugeon's care and lack of tolerance. This issue hardly is the proper place to find these modern racers.

But the subjects of this column are grizzled graybeards-among their brethren, cut-down coupes among a corps of Troyer Cavaliers. These are some of racing's elder statesmen, the men to which runny-nosed rookies should look for guidance before heading out on their first misadventures.

Such is the passage of time. At one point in their careers, a long-gone point in time, these graybeards were towheads themselves, looking for guidance from the very legends about which you will read in this magazine. The lessons learned over 30 years of competition have come hard, and most lessons started with just the sort of misadventures that will be witnessed at any bullring on any weekend this summer as new rookies begin their own education.

Ask even the best and most experienced racer in the region to recall the first time he turned a wheel in competition and the story invariably begins with a stifled chuckle and a sigh of resignation. It'll also serve notice that even for racing's legends the sport's lessons were learned the hard way, including its first, seemingly obvious one.

"It's a lot different from the grandstands," relates longtime modified pilot Bob Potter, reciting this first lesson. "It was just another world from being in the pits."

Potter had viewed the other world from outside the third-turn fence at Waterford Speedbowl, where the former Speedbowl Modified champion made his racing debut almost 30 years ago in the Bowl's old Bomber division. Waterford's Bombers allowed cars to run six-cylinder GM power, or the once ubiquitous Ford flatheads. Potter's car ran the latter mill.

"(It had) triple carbs and aluminum heads and it was bored and stroked; it was an old Danbury car. I got a heck of a deal on it.

"When I went out there the first time I thought I was flying," Potter then recalls of his first laps in his new machine, which were turned during one of Waterford's open practices. "All of a sudden I heard this roaring thunder coming by me. It was Dick Beauregard. He won, like, 24 or 25 races that year. That really shocked me. My foot started going 'bub, bub, bub' on the throttle. I said 'C'mon foot! Calm down!' But I was all right after that."

Potter, who has stepped back from regular competition this season to take stock while he tends to his ailing brother, and can't remember how he finished in his first race later that evening other than to admit, "I guess I didn't do too well," agrees with the initial observation of this story.

"It was just a learning factor. We didn't know nothing about racing."

Pete Fiandaca knew a little. He'd campaigned his own cars with others at the wheel before he ever headed out onto the track himself.

"I always wanted to drive," he says, "so when the right time came I did it."

The right time came in1967 at the old Westboro Speedway, after he got his hands on a car prepared for Westboro's B Division.

"I ran a '49 Ford Coupe," he says. "I had bought the car for $35 and I pretty much ran it as it was."

Don't ask Fiandaca to recall details about his first attempt as a driver. For him, only one overriding memory remains, and it speaks for itself.

"l was the slowest car out there."

If anything, Russ Wood's – ahem – "debut" was even more inauspicious.

"We had been to Hudson a few times with my father," he says, remembering back over 20 years. "One Saturday we had the idea we'd take a Rookie Stock there.

"It was an old Chrysler four-door. We took the windows out and took a spray bomb and put numbers on it. We borrowed a trailer from a guy and we towed it with my half-ton van."

Wood and his brother loaded their new racecar on the trailer tail-first and headed out for Hudson, ready for their first racing adventure. It didn't come at the track.

"We got about a half-mile from my house. Evidently we didn't tie the car down real good. It ended up rolling forward, and the crank on the front of the trailer tore a hole in the gas tank. Luckily I was able to turn it around and head back home. So it was an exciting weekend."

So was the next one, when Wood finally made it to Hudson, only to struggle with a car, the performance of which, to put Wood's description euphemistically, duplicated the odor of human excrement.

This season Wood will again run the full ISMA schedule with the focused professional, first-class Paul Dunigan racing operation. That's led to somewhat of a change in perspective since Wood's first days as a racer.

"This was the big-time for us," he laughs, "being in the pits at Hudson!"

Not everyone struggles their first time out. Most make it to the racetrack, for one thing. Some even run okay once they get there. Like Bobby Gahan. His story starts typically, in a B-Division racecar, at Star Speedway in his case.

"I traded a Triumph motorcycle for it," says Gahan. "It was, like, a '32 Plymouth coupe. It was like the supermods with Buick motors, but they called them cutdowns.

"It went pretty good. I wasn't a world-beater, but I finished top five. It was a good day."

That qualifies more as a great day for a new racer. Still, Gahan, who, having lost patience with the politics of the sport, expects to return as a weekly racer to Star this season, acknowledges the challenge he faced as a rookie in the mid-'50s.

"It was a lot of fury but it was difficult to learn to run with those cars."

Maine veteran Ralph Nason also went pretty well right out of the box. He just didn't go well long enough to get a decent finish out of it. Nason, who plans to run a partial schedule with the Pro All-Star Series this season, was a distributor for Wynn's during the early '60s. He was advised at the time to check racing out as a potential customer-base. So he went to Unity Speedrway, which he now owns, with friend and business-colleague Wayne Philbrook. Philbrook soon betrayed an ignorance of the first lesson of racing, the one related previously here by Potter.

"Wayne said 'Let's get a car,'" Nason explained. "'It looks like they're having a good time.'"

The duo got their hands on a car, and Philbrook took a stab behind the wheel.

"I didn't want to do it," admits Nason with a laugh.

Philbrook realized within a few weeks that the appearance of "fun" in racing can be deceiving, and so he gave up the seat – not to Nason but to another driver. That driver did no better than Philbrook, even after Nason and Philbrook provided him with a new car, even after Nason's father massaged the car's ignition system in a quest for more power, even after Nason had the car going 90 mph in second gear on a dirt road near his home.

"So I put a helmet on and got in it," says Nason of how he

impulsively entered his first race. "I started last, and in three laps I'd passed the whole field. I think I put it up in the banks after that. But it had the power."

Paul Richardson's first race was equally forgettable. He started out in 1965 at the old Pines Speedway, in that track's Bomber division. When he first got out on the quarter-mile Groveland oval, his heart started racing before his car did.

"I was pretty happy," he says, "but I was horrified.

"I started toward the front, and we were all lined up on the track. I looked in the mirror and right there I wondered if I'd done the right thing. All I saw was bumpers and fenders and the faces of guys who wanted to get by me.

"When the green flag fell all hell broke loose. I didn't finish. I crashed; I'll admit it. But I crashed because I was totally unprepared."

But Richardson, who's easing into racing retirement beginning this year, also was thrilled by the experience. And beyond the first lesson of what a different world it was out on the track, Richardson came away from his first race with a second lesson learned.

"After that I just looked ahead of me," he says. "I didn't look behind me anymore.

"You know, before that year was out I'd won a race. Do you believe it? I won a g*damned race."

In retrospect it's easy to believe that of Richardson or of any of these guys. Once they'd put that first race behind them none of them were looking back.

LEW BOYD

From the Lowell Sun, *2004. Lew Boyd continues to share memories of racing's early days through his website, Coastal 181. Check it out to learn more about some of racing's greatest drivers from some of its best writers.*

Among the memorable characters who wrote the history of New England shorttrack racing with their exploits, Lew Boyd is uniquely equipped to put the stories to paper.

Decades ago racing in the region was dominated by a cadre of earthy adventurers who lived for the day. These local legends didn't think much beyond the racetrack to which they were towing the open trailers containing crude machines cobbled together out of bits of junk and pounds of welding rod. They lived for the moment, damning tomorrow as dismissively as they forgot yesterday.

Lew Boyd was one of them. He traveled the state-routes and back roads of the Northeast, racecar in tow, living in the day-to-day world of the barnstorming racer. But Boyd also developed a long view of life dismissed by his colleagues. He studied hard, graduated from Harvard, and developed a career in the longview world of management-consulting.

Ultimately Boyd realized that a compelling folklore had developed around his old heroes and more recent contemporaries. He also realized his perspective on life as well as racing, not to mention his classical education, put him in perfect position to record the region's racing's history. More than that, though, he realized it was another opportunity to enjoy the contrast racing provided to his chosen career.

``It's really a pleasure to be dealing with racing people,'' Boyd declared Monday from his Newburyport office. ``There's a real basic truth to racing. You know, you either win or you don't.''

Boyd's avocation within an avocation has led him to recently write "Hot Cars Cool Drivers," a history of three now defunct but once thriving racetracks in the area, Groveland's Pines Speedway as well as Norwood Arena and Westboro Speedway.

``I'm trying to record back to a time when activities went on that just couldn't go on now,'' Boyd explained, ``that were so spirited, so outrageous, and just so neat!''

Despite Boyd's pedigree, his is no ``Paper Lion'' story of one of the Harvard elite discovering the dignity among the working class.

``It actually predates Harvard,'' Boyd agreed. ``I was born in upstate New York. To use a psychological term, I was `imprinted' with racing at a very early age. We didn't grow up wishing to be baseball players. We grew up wanting to be dirt-track racers.''

After moving to Cambridge, Boyd got his wish.

``I started my racing career at Hudson (NH) and Westboro,'' he recalled. ``Then after college I started taking the Mass Pike out to New York.''

The love of dirt-racing, ingrained in Boyd's New York childhood, remains.

``Much of the racing I do now, and I don't do much, is dirt,'' he declares, before admitting, ``I will say after 42 years the young drivers are getting awfully fast and don't have much respect for my hair color.''

It's not the drivers who have come after Boyd that inspired him to write a number of books about the Northeast's racing history, it was the ones who came before him, and as he related, one in particular.

``I got a call from Kenny Shoemaker. He'd helped me so much in the early '70s. He said he was dying, and he was trying to get a book done. I told him he'd had such an impact on me if there was something I could do I would. So he sent me a bunch of tapes he had made.'

180

And Boyd went to work on his first book.

``One of my proudest moments," he declared, ``was getting that book done before he died."

The motivation was the same with his latest work.

``I knew we had to do something because some of these guys are on their last laps."

DAVE DION GETS REAL

From the Attleboro Sun Chronicle, 2002. Yes, you've read about Dave, and you've read about Seekonk. But it's my favorite racetrack as described by one of my favorite drivers. Deal with it.

It's been a memorable ride for NASCAR's Busch North Series the past two weekends. Superspeedways at Loudon, N.H. and Nazareth, Pa., television cameras and famous commentators in the TV booth, motorhomes in the infield, photo finishes, celebrity grand marshals and the other uptown touches of NASCAR's popularity in today's sports world.

But the Busch North Series teams and fans never forget their shorttrack roots, and this Saturday night will produce blue collar racing at its best when the series returns to one of its original home tracks, the Seekonk Speedway.

Known as the Cement Palace, the wide, nearly-circular one-third mile oval on Route 6 between Providence, R.I., and Fall River, Mass., is ringed by concrete stands that bring the term "bullring" to mind in its most positive sense. That's especially true when they're filled with savvy and enthusiastic racefans who appreciate the artistry of racing full-bodied stock cars at close quarters.

The only Busch North race of the 2002 season at Seekonk is the

182

Budweiser 150, scheduled to take the green flag this Saturday. A full program in Seekonk's regular NASCAR Weekly Racing Series presented by Dodge will accompany the Budweiser 150.

No one is a harder competitor, or a more articulate spokesman for shorttrack racing than Dave Dion. For over 30 years has been slinging orange Fords prepared by his brother Roger around New England's oval tracks. In 1996 he won the Busch North Series championship, and in 2000 he scored a memorable triumph as the series returned to Seekonk after a 13-year absence. The victory-lane photo of Dion with speedway owner Mrs. Irene Venditti – two of the most recognized faces in New England stock car racing – is one of the images which define Busch North racing.

Showing just how narrow the line is between the proverbial thrill of victory and agony of defeat, Dion could manage only 12th in the 2001 edition of the Budweiser 150, although he rebounded to fourth in the series' midsummer return to Seekonk last year. "We went back last year coming off a win the year before, and we found out how tough it is," he said with a chuckle. "All those people who we were lapping the year before; I know now what they felt like."

Since 150 laps at Seekonk amounts to one sweeping, 50-mile left turn, the physical demands are daunting. The driver's arms, shoulders, and especially the neck are under constant strain. "It's not as bad today in a Busch North car with a good head restraint," Dion noted, recalling that it wasn't always that way: "I saw George Summers pull out when he was leading a modified race. I asked him if the motor blew and he said, 'No, my head fell off!'"

Along with driver-skill, patience, and stamina, Seekonk calls for a racecar that handles. Scheduled pit stops aren't practical, since the pit-area is located outside turns three and four, connected to the track by tunnels under the grandstand. The car that rolls off the line is the car that has to be competitive 150 laps later. That puts the premium on experience and chassis-setup, one reason why the three Busch North Series races at Seekonk since 2000 have been won by Dave Dion, Kelly Moore and Dale Shaw – three of the series's smartest and toughest veterans.

"You don't need any horsepower. You don't need any aerodynamics.

You don't need any brakes," Dave Dion stressed when asked about the winning combination at Seekonk. Proudly he added, "There's no excuse for the blue-collar teams not to go to Seekonk and run well in that race. The money-teams have absolutely no advantage."

That's enough to make Dave Dion, perhaps the ultimate blue-collar racer active in 2002, welcome the challenge of Seekonk. But there's one more attraction that makes the Cement Palace irresistible to him.

"It's up close and personal with the fans."

THE PRODIGAL CHARLIE ROSE

From Late Model Racer, *2003. See? Not everybody likes Seekonk as much as I do. But they all return.*

It used to be racers just raced. There were no master plans. There were no marketing deals, no sponsorship-proposals. There were no PR reps writing much about nothing, looking to generate buzz. There were no concerns about projecting an image, no attending seminars, no appointments at Hair Club for Men.

There just were countless hours spent in florescent-lit garages out behind the house, and trips to racetracks with trailers in tow. And there was racing, plenty of racing, never as a means to the next level but simply racing as a means to living the moment, really living it, this moment right *here*, and then reliving it over a couple of cold ones before heading home and calling it a night.

But those racers still exist. Of course they do. You know the ones at your home track. They've been towing there for years, and they're there every week. They don't quit just because they don't get to move on. They don't say goodbye to racing altogether just because the sponsorship-deal never comes along, or because the media never starts to hum with the buzz of their names. And they don't move on. They arrive every week because the gates are swung open every week and every week there's a new race to be won and a new chance to shine and fresh cold ones to quaff. And with all of that a new life to live, every Saturday night.

Charlie Rose, Jr., is one of those racers. He's too old to play that, ``When I grow up I'm going to be a Winston Cup hero," game. He's too savvy and self-assured, and comfortable in his own skin, to put up with all that. And he's way too young to quit playing the game the way he's always played it, and the way his father played it before him.

Besides, he's still winning. Rose just snared his third pro stock title up at New Hampshire's Star Speedway, his third driving for the ready, willing and Able Motorsports. And his plans for 2003 are for more of the same, more battling against the same solid corps of competitors on the same bent and warped little quarter-mile oval that has sent some racers screaming into the night (not to mention into the woods surrounding half the track).

He did move on, though, at least in a manner of speaking. The elder Charlie Rose made his name down the road a piece, at the legendary quarter-mile circle of concrete in eastern Massachusetts, Seekonk Speedway. That's the path down which Rose and the Able team started, and Seekonk represented a home track they didn't plan to leave. Then it rained. While most of the teams loading up in Seekonk's pits pointed the haulers back toward the garage behind the house, the Able team collectively decided to head in another direction seeking more new moments on the racetrack, more living than can enjoyed back at the garage on a race night.

``We called Star," recalls Able chief mechanic Glenn Mattos, ``and they were running."

And Star welcomed the strangers with open arms.

``We pulled up to the gate," says Rose, ``and they said 'The second heat goes out in five minutes. If you can make it go on out.' We pulled the car out of the trailer, went out and started dead last."

Study the inconsistencies between Star's and Seekonk's pro stock rules, and you'll understand that Rose didn't have a snowball's chance in Pamela Anderson's underwear of running strongly that night. But the impression had been made. These outsiders were welcome here. In nine years the welcome hasn't worn off, even as Rose drove to his third title this past season. And that's saying something, because racing at Star hardly is tip-toeing through tulips. Star punishes carelessness; there's just enough of an outside line there to tempt impatient pro stock drivers but not enough to reward them. More likely they'll find themselves running out of room as they slide off Star's flight deck of a backstraight or try to hold it together through its slick turns three and four, where they'll come upon a front-stretch wall that seems to cross their path.

Yet this NASCAR Weekly Racing Series division is rich in talent and experience, including the likes of 2001 division-champion Dan Bezanson and grizzled greybeard racer Bobby Gahan, who returned to the weekly wars at Star this season after fleeing the sinking ship that was the Pro Stock division at nearby Lee USA Speedway. These guys share a grudging respect for one another, nurtured by the experience that comes from years of going at each other at a place where one's stupidity can spell disaster for many others.

``Guys know things happen on a racetrack," explains Rose. ``That's where you have to leave it. A lot of times you can't even tell what really happened from where you were sitting. You think you didn't do anything wrong and then when you see (the video) later you realize you didn't really see what went on.

``But it's really the same at any racetrack," he maintains. ``Out-and-out take-outs, you don't see much of that anywhere. But you can't show up having any feelings."

And with a group of veterans such as Star enjoys there's nothing to lose by being open-minded. These guys have earned their stripes, if not their purple hearts. There's nothing left to prove by mimicking the nonsense to which street-stock rookies routinely subject each other. Besides, there's no need to point fingers. Everyone at Star from Rose down to the kid playing with Hot Wheels behind the stands knows disaster is always just a corner away for any driver on the track.

``It's so small you just know that something's going to happen," says Rose. ``You just don't know when."

That's what makes Rose's 2002 title run so amazing. Forget wins and podium finishes, Mattos points out a better way to measure the success of the Able team. Just look at the Able car, which is financed and fielded by Mattos's brother Gary.

``We replaced one fender all year," he declares with a measure of pride. ``That's it. And that's because an A-frame broke."

There's more to be gained from a veteran's perspective than the simple realization that ``shit happens." There also is the healthy point of view that racing for racing's sake as opposed to racing as part of some larger, more ambitous agenda can bring its own rewards no matter what the final finish is. Rose articulates the theory eloquently.

``(Racing) is self-challenging, not only to beat the other guys, but to see how much better you can do yourself. Besides, if you finish tenth but you were racing with ten good cars, and you got stuck on the outside for 30 laps and you made up an inch, you get out and know `Hey, that was fun.' "

More pro stock drivers could benefit from such an attitude. Despite new opportunities for pro-stock level drivers in New England, such as the Pro Stock All-Star Series and the American Canadian Tour, this still is a racers' division. Which means if you're looking to make some money – sell your car. On the other hand, if you're looking to win pro stock races, sell everything else you own, because winning will take a level of commitment that boarders on Obsessive-Compulsive Disorder.

``Too many tracks don't pay enough," says Rose. ``It has to be gratifying. That's why there are only four or five guys at every track who run at the front. They're the ones able to do what they need to do. They have the time they're willing to put in. Their families understand this is what they do – or they have no families."

Next season the Able team's OCD behavior will become even more serious and will require even more understanding from the families affected. Even as their primary car gets renewed for the new Star season, a second Distance Racing chassis is being readied for selected shows on the PASS tour. Both cars are quality pieces, built to Distance's stout standards and powered by engines that came together in the more than capable hands of motor-master Nat Chievattone. It must be noted, however, that the team is limited to the horses a modest engine-budget allows.

``That's the biggest thing for us," admits mechanic Mattos. ``We just don't have the pieces to build competitive motors. We'll stick to the

(PASS) tracks where horsepower isn't the big thing."

Weekly visits to Star will continue to fit that bill as well. Unfortunately, what might be a modestly funded team's best option for traveling, occasional visits to compete against the regulars in someone else's weekly series, is not an option in provincial New England, where promoters seem to think good confusion about rules makes good neighbors. That philosophy of writing rules that make visits to other weekly-series tracks pointless leaves Mattos scratching his head.

``If they made rules the same but kept you happy why would you go someplace else?'' he asks rhetorically.

For Mattos, Rose, and Able Motorsports, there'd be only one reason. To race, and therefore to live.

THE MISADVENTURES OF DALE QUARTERLY

From Shorttrack Magazine, *2004. Despite how this might read here, it turns out his teammates were* not *impressed.*

It wasn't the 24 Hours of Le Mans, only the 24 Hours of Nelson Ledges, a motorcycle race of endurance on a club track in Ohio.

Sure, it was serious competition – for many. But not for everyone. Certainly not, for instance, for the team that annually campaigned a Vespa scooter, providing a rolling chicane for other riders of widely disparate talent.

For Dale Quarterley, then a young lion among a horde of skilled and crazy motorcycle roadracers, it was a race, which to him meant only one thing, ride as if there were no tomorrow, even though tomorrow was when the race would end. Quarterley had been recruited as the anchor on a team that was a microcosm of the race itself, made up of grimly-focused national-level riders as well as affable amateurs.

"I'm at a track I've never been to before on a bike I've never been on before," he recalls two decades later, "and I'm the fastest guy on the team."

Which meant that the more laps Quarterley was on the team's bone-stock Suzuki, the better the chance the team could win the race. And as darkness fell on Nelson Ledges the formula became more pronounced.

"I was a half-second slower at night," he contends. "Everybody else was two seconds slower. They said, 'This is a no-brainer.'"

Of course they meant having Quarterley ride every other shift was a no-brainer. For Quarterley, intent on winning above all else, it ended up meaning that their chances were even better if he just stayed on the bike all night. Which he proceeded to do, literally refusing to get off even when he came in to refuel.

"I was cruising, and I wasn't even wearing myself out, although I was physically."

More accurately, Quarterley was not aware of how dehydrated he was becoming. Wasn't aware right up to the point where he began to wobble like a top about to go over before doing exactly that in a cloud of dust, taking both the team's quite comfortable overall and production-class leads with him.

But it wasn't in Quarterley to quit. Barely conscious, he got back on the bent bike and made his way to the pits, where Johnny Gray, later a national endurance-series champion, went out to reclaim the production victory and a fourth overall. Quarterley was taken to the hospital, where a doctor patched up two broken legs and a hand injury while keeping him conscious with deliberate chatter ("Explain to me again how you got grass under here.").

Quarterley made it back to the track in time to mount the podium with the aid of his team, which, in fine motorcycle-roadracing tradition, was highly amused by the whole incident.

If you can understand and appreciate that sense of amusement you might begin to comprehend how Dale Quarterley's sense of "100 percent" might be a few points higher than many of his competitors in NASCAR's Busch North. It's a good lesson for some young racers who will tell you they're at 100 percent all the time in their pro stock or midget and they'll be at 100 percent right past the point they land a Busch North ride. It's a good lesson, too, for the competitors who accuse Quarterley of the crime of being – ahem – aggressive.

"I agree," says Quarterley. "I am aggressive. I do push the envelope. Once in a while I get in trouble. But guys will come up to me after we get together. I say to them 'You tell me how many times in the last ten to twenty races I've gotten in an accident and I went into the pits torn up from doing something.' My point is that in most cases it was a racing incident. (I was) running 100 percent and the guy next to me was running 100 percent and he couldn't handle it."

In a land of racing cliches, another one, "Ask no quarter, give none," immediately comes to mind. But if the shoe fits...

"I don't hang people. I give them options. It might not be the options they want, but they have options.

"It was like at Loudon. I heard people complaining about our being three-wide. I'm saying "What is your problem? I was the one on the outside.'"

And no wonder he's not complaining. It's likely his heart-rate was hardly elevated, not after racing on a motorcycle.

"You go into a corner at Brainard or Elkhart Lake and pitch it over at 160 and your footpeg's dragging and you're wobbling and there's a guy right next to you doing the same thing; that's exhilarating.

"Here you get together with somebody and you end up in the wall, you throw it in reverse and keep going.'"

So, you still saying you were at 100 percent?

SUPER VIC

From Shortrack Magazine, *2003. You already know I love guys like Vic Miller. Read why here.*

In these days of crate-engines and body-templates, fewer and fewer racing series provide fertile ground for creative car builders.

In shorttrack racing, a supermodified is the last refuge for creative iconoclasts. With a super the builder's imagination can seem the only limit, the only template constraining creative vision.

If it's ever been done on a shorttrack it's been done to a super. Drivers have worked from behind, in front of and next to massive fuel-injected big-blocks. Wings have been ahead of them, behind them, over their heads, and even all around them. Radiators have migrated similarly and at various degrees of horizontal and vertical. Cars have utilized every combination of shock, coil and bar, suspension-components extending in every direction.

Fans of supers often have as much fun trolling the pits as they do watching the racing. It can appear to the casual eye that no two supermods are alike. Certainly the front-runners in an International SuperModified Association event present wildly divergent approaches to the challenge of breaking the sound-barrier in a barrel. Watch supers race long enough, and you'll notice that some teams present a variety of wildly divergent approaches all by themselves.

Then there's Vic Miller. Vic Miller is the iconoclast of iconoclasts. While all around him others are losing their heads (or at least leaning them over at every angle) Miller, driver Chris Perley, and the Miller team approach ISMA racing with a strategy that could come straight out of the owner's manual for a Legends car.

Miller's approach begins with a straightforward chassis-design proven over countless seasons of competition. The design has produced volumes of setup information, which in turn serves as a resource for careful and deliberate application of proven principles as well as occasional leaps of faith in the face of poor results. It's an approach that works.

"We really have to work hard to screw it up," declares Miller as he, Perley and the Miller team surround two almost identical supers sitting in the basement-shop of Miller's modest ranch house in southern New Hampshire.

The two cars are the most recent in a line of machines that have evolved slowly over decades of competition.

"There have just been subtle changes," Miller says. "We might move something a little to the left, a little to the right."

Even those minor adjustments don't get made casually. Miller's a veteran of the ISMA wars. He's been around long enough to know the difference between "change" and "improvement." That's why he takes a hard look at any idea before he incorporates it into his cars. After all, any modification to a proven design negates all those volumes of data. There's enough change at any racetrack – not only season to season, but hour to hour – so why change the tool you're using to figure a track out?

"If you're off with one of these there's no way a driver can compensate," Miller explains. "They're so overpowered. If you're a little off you're spinning tires or burning them off before the race is over."

Winning races by preserving tires might seem a tame way to win races in the untamed monster a super is, but as supers have grown more insane sanity has grown more important. When you have 800 horses in a 1,700-pound car, you're more interested in holding the

194

reins tight than in unleashing the beast. Chris Perley understands this.

"He's real smooth," says Miller. "He drives in and he picks the throttle up just right. He's really worked out. He's, like, the perfect guy for us."

This perfect relationship is particularly productive in practice, when ISMA teams have limited opportunity to solve the mysteries not only of heat-races often run under a baking sun but features going green on cooler pavement hours later. The Miller team has learned to focus on a couple of areas and bring the weight of its experience to the effort.

"We work with the springs and the crossweight mostly," says Miller, admitting, "You can get yourself so messed up."

He's especially intent on avoiding band-aid approaches. Don't go looking for Miller to start playing with wing-angles, for instance, to try to find grip that suspension-changes are not delivering.

"You can see the marks on the body where the wings line up," Miller notes, pointing to the nose-wings on one car. "You can almost just line them up when you bolt them on."

Having a long history matching car to track also improves the process of preparing for features that won't start until hours later. You might consider that the team is focused more on the end of the night than the laps leading up to it. Miller's preoccupation with saving tires is one example. That they can accept less than perfect heat-race results is another.

"It just seems like for some reason these cars don't run good during the day," says Miller.

"If we run well in the heat we're screwed!" adds Chris Perley with a laugh, before explaining, "We always make a change between the heat and the feature..."

"But it's never enough," laughs Miller.

Sometimes it isn't. Sometimes caution must be thrown to the wind, even by the deliberate Miller. He cites as one example the team's struggles at Sandusky over the years and what turned things around there last season.

"We'd be out there going 'What do you want to do?' 'I dunno, what do *you* want to do?' We pulled out setups from, like, ten years ago. (Chris) didn't like it at first, but I told him, 'What could be worse? Maybe instead of running tenth let's run 20th and get out of here early!"

No such luck.

"We had half a lap on the field (in the feature) until we broke a heim-rod end."

Such a story is the exception to the rule, born of desperation after a day of struggle. It's more illustrative to consider that Miller's two racecars (as well as the car Rick Wentworth built as a copy of the Miller cars and drove to victory at Seekonk last year) are of the supposedly obsolete four-bar design.

"I think we're the only ones running them," says Miller. "But I think I really know this design, and I know what works with them.

"That's why we might drop off and somebody might do really well maybe for a year or two. But I've been up and down more times."

And through those up-and-down times Miller has learned one thing, one thing that never changes, whether you're up or down.

"Oval-track racing is always the same," he explains. "All the guys who are going fast are going fast through the turns. I don't care what it is, Winston Cup or supermods. All the guys winning are going fast through the turns."

Chris Perley is doing both, in a car-design long ago rejected as obsolete.

The more things change...

TC

From Trackside Magazine, *2000. In August of 2017 Ted Christopher died in a private plane crash on his way to a modified race at Riverhead New York. A line in this story is sadly and eerily prescient.*

...the more they stay the same.

Just wanted to finish the thought I started when I closed my column in last month's *Trackside.* That column ended with comments concerning the omnipresent Ted Christopher, who seemed to be popping up every time I turned around. And it's only gotten more noticable since that column was published.

You've probably witnessed this yourself if you've been doing any race-chasing in southern New England. If there are modifieds of any stripe racing anywhere, you can be sure Ted Christopher is in one of them. He's also climbed into a couple of Busch cars – North and South – and probably is the guy who knocked over your grandmother when he went racing through the neighborhood on a BMX bike.

I began to wonder both why Christopher was spreading himself so thin and why there were so few others who raced this much. Of course it used to be that plenty of guys raced all week. But years ago if you built a modified you could take it anywhere. The cars came together relatively cheaply, especially if you or your buddy owned a junkyard, and you towed it behind your trusty pickup.

Add to that the fact that a big race was 50 laps, maybe 100, but short enough in any case that piles of expensive tires didn't need to be factored into the equation. Or more precisely – what equation? Guys just towed their cars to racetracks until they ran out of money. Then they put their last beer between their legs, fired up the pickup, and towed home.

These days everybody has a plan, advancing through a ``career" one rung at a time, never losing sight of the top rung even if their feet keep missing the ones they're trying to climb on. Every step is deliberate, their focus never wavers, and the climbers remain grimly determined to move in only one direction.

In the meantime a few guys keep getting in the way. They insist on jumping around all over every ladder. Just when you go to step up they jump from the ladder next to you onto the rung you're heading for. Then they jump back again, or onto a different ladder. Sometimes they step down a rung – or two! And they don't even care! Look – they're smiling! Don't they even have a plan?

Ted Christopher isn't into rungs, he's into racing. He doesn't even think about the consequences of spreading himself thin. He's more focused on minimizing the number of waking moments spent outside a racecar.

``I always like it when it's like this," he admits of his current schedule. ``I guess I like to race."

It should be no surprise that Christopher started racing in karts. It's typical in karting, where a dozen or more different classes may hold races in one event, for karters to run a bunch of different classes to maximize seat-time. It's an easy proposition because many classes differ only in minimum weight allowed, so light guys like Christopher simply bolt on a few more pounds to make the next green flag. Or guys will load a couple more karts in the trailer. They're small enough.

``I remember one year I went to the Woodstock Fair," Chistopher recalls of the Labor Day fair in northeastern Connecticut that hosts a weekend of kart racing. The shows attract karters the way the more notorious Woodstock attracted mosquitos. ``I ran 17 features in three days – and won 15 of them."

198

The dye was cast. When Christopher started racing stock cars the idea of hitting Stafford and Thompson every week must have seemed like a no-brainer. C'mon, there were *days* between shows. He was used to minutes. Later Waterford was added to form the tri-track series and Christopher simply took it in stride. He's continued to do that as opportunities have presented themselves. And his criteria for taking advantage of them has remained a constant from his karting days. Can the car being offered win races? In the last few years he's answered in the affirmative more than ever.

``The last three years have been great," he agrees. ``I'm in really good equipment right now. I have the potential to win every time I go out."

He goes out more than Richard Gere did in American Gigolo. He's driven three different Featherlite Modifieds this season, his own, Joe Brady's and Gary Cretty's. SK Mod races have been run in his car as well as Jim Galente's. Randy Lajoie has provided a Busch North ride at New Hampshire, Stafford and on the series's road courses. He's also set to drive in the series for Glenn Rudolph. And don't forget the drive he took in a Busch Grand National car owned by Michael Waltrip.

Crews line his cars up as if he were in charge of valet parking. He won a Busch North race at Stafford in June, made nice with two interviewers, smiled a lot with different ballcaps on, and then climbed into his SK and went out and won the nightcap. When Stafford held twin SK features Christopher won both of them.

Later at Thompson Christopher won right out of the box in his first race for Cretty and then again won the SK – er, Sunoco – Mod race. Meanwhile parents at Thompson's adjacent Little-T Speedway have asked Don Hoenig not to schedule races for Sunday because they fear Christopher will climb into a Quarter-Midget and blow away a horde of petulant 12-year olds.

Okay, I made that one up, but you get the picture.

Don't ask what series take priority. That's what air travel is for. In June he qualified in the BGN car at Watkins Glen and then flew back to New England to drive in the Featherlite Tour race at Seekonk Speedway.

You might wonder how Christopher keeps track of all these cars and the peculiarity of each, not to mention the vastly different demands of modified versus late model racing.

``When I went from the Busch North to the SK Mod it was like a high-speed video game, it was so much faster. If I run the SK first I especially have to slow down."

Christopher admits this ain't the way a modern driver is supposed to conduct himself, but he's not typical of modern drivers. He doesn't see how heading ``Down South" would necessarily improve his racing. He's also evidently not big on the charm-school theory of driver conduct.

``I expect that if something came along I would take it. But I'm not going to sit around kissing somebody's ass. And I don't have five million dollars to spend."

Christopher reiterates his appreciation of the top-shelf cars he currently races.

``Do I want to go down there and run 60 percent?" he asks.

It would be unfair to imply that anybody who races in more than one division is conceding his future in racing. Jerry Marquis has been competing in as many divisions as Christopher, even if he's done it with just three race teams. But he's proven to be the exception that proves the ``one driver – one plan" rule. Marquis planned to focus on the Busch North series, as is typical of drivers looking to promote their careers beyond New England. When sponsorship-woes hit Busch North car owner Tony Vecchio, Marquis accepted a ride from Featherlite Mod owner Mario Fiore. Even then the plan was to concentrate on the BN series and fit the SK, owned by Rob Chawansky and Joe Santoro, into the picture when possible.

Then Marquis muddied the water up by winning back-to-back races in Fiore's potent machine. Since then he's been dancing between tracks, continuing with Vecchio's rejuvenated effort and trying to get as many races in as possible in the hopes that success can be defined three ways.

``We've got our plates pretty full," he admits. ``It's a pretty tough schedule."

Talk to Marquis and you realize that his plan remains. It's just been, shall we say, ``modified."

``We're still looking to move down south. I'm looking to prove myself. I'm just doing it in three different fashions."

One of those fashions, Marquis would have to admit, must be in a Busch car, where recognition is maximized and success can best be applied to NASCAR's higher levels. Not that Marquis necessarily is thrilled with that, apparently.

``The modifieds are a lot of fun to drive," he declares. ``The Busch North cars are very demanding because of the finesse you need.

``But I think it's good for me. It sharpens your pencil. It gives me a lot more seat time."

The difference between Marquis and Christopher, then, is that Marquis sees seat time as a means to an end. To Christopher, it is an end. While Marquis must know he will need to devote himself down south as much to his time outside his racecar as his time in it, signing autographs, waving and smiling, and answering more stupid questions from people like me than he ever has before, Christopher wants as little of that as possible.

In a series made up of young drivers like Tony Stewart, who has struggled to learn the kiss-ass art of stock car superstar, there isn't much room for a guy like Ted Christopher.

Imagine a racing series about which you have to say that.

PAUL DUNIGAN

From the Lowell Sun, *2004. An interesting – and unapologetic – guy.*

Some people are just bigger than the rest of us. Sometimes that's obvious. They tower over those of us of average height. Doorways are not large enough to let them pass without bending over. Low ceilings prevent them from standing erect.

For others, their large stature cannot be measured in inches. Still, they seem to fill a room, with the size of their personality, with the force of their will, or with the flamboyance of their personal style. Or their voice fills it as it booms from wall to wall. Perhaps it's simply their ego that seems to loom so large. Whatever the measure, they just seem bigger than the rest of us.

It might be hard to define exactly what it was that made Paul Dunigan such a larger-than-life character, but all of the above criteria seemed to apply. Dunigan, who succumbed to cancer in April, appeared large in stature, but it was the way he lived a life so huge that defined him more than his appearance, broad shoulders and flamboyantly flowing white mane notwithstanding.

As a racer Dunigan played large. His was the biggest team in the fastest series that calls New England home. The Dunigan supermodifieds won a number of International Supermodified Association titles. He employed some of the sport's greatest shorttrack

202

drivers, men like Bentley Warren, Russ Wood, Joe Gosek and Mike Ordway. It wasn't unusual to see the team field three or more cars in a race in a series where few teams could afford to field more than one. And each car would be prepared by Landmark crew-chief Brian Allegresso to a level of perfection few teams could duplicate.

All of this combined to create in Dunigan an ``overdog'' stature bound to cause resentment among the lesser-endowed supermod teams. It was easy to label Dunigan as the George Steinbrenner of super racing as he brought together resources in equipment and personnel few other teams could match. Yet Paul Dunigan made no apologies.

``These are the fastest, most expensive cars racing around here,'' he asserted once. ``If they can't afford to race them they should go race street stocks.''

Indeed Dunigan seemed to enjoy his ``evil empire'' status. All of it, however, was just part of the fun of racing for him. The truth of the matter was he enjoyed racing just as much – maybe more – when his cars didn't dominate. A few years ago this writer contacted Dunigan after his team, defending the ISMA championship for the umpteenth consecutive time, got a off to a slow start that ultimately cost them the title. Of course, he grumbled about his team's early-season misfortunes, but he roared with laughing approval when asked about the performances of the competitors who led him in points.

``I think it's great!'' he declared. ``It's about time those guys quit complaining and figured out how to beat us.''

It wasn't as easily discernable, but Dunigan's heart was a large part of his large personality. While he quietly helped others in need, the rides he provided for drivers in need of a break were the most obvious examples of his nature. This season that generosity was to be extended to young phenom Jon McKennedy after the Chelmsford teenager proved his talents by winning Star Speedway's 350 Super title last season.

The future of the Landmark Racing team is up in the air at the present time. That's no surprise, because undoubtedly right now, whatever the financial and logistical crisis Allegresso and the rest of the Landmark Racing team faces, the absence of Paul Dunigan looms as large in his Lowell race shop as his presence ever did.

I WISH I'D MET HIM

From Trackside Magazine, *1995. Just one of a ton of special people in racing.*

The first time Dean Nardi asked me, it was an assignment. The second time, it was to satisfy my own curiosity. Twice I called Frank Procopio to try to get him to agree to talk to me for a story in *Trackside*. The first time, he explained to me that it just wasn't a good time for him, and he wasn't really of a mind to talk about racing.

Fair enough. But I wondered, what's the big deal? I wasn't Ted Koppel. I just wanted to talk racing with a guy who'd seen a lot of it. But I resigned myself to the fact that he was not interested in talking with some stranger, at least not then. I figured I would forget it and, in typical preoccupied writer's style, I went looking for my next assignment.

A year or so went by, and I began thinking, again like a writer, that it might be smart to check in with Frank. I figured things would be fine and I'd have this great angle on some sort of racing recovery or something. An example of someone who'd found some truths left over from racing that applied in a bigger way to life in general, maybe. A story, you know?

No. No story, and not because the time wasn't right. This time it was just, well just because.

Well, I was more puzzled than ever, but this time I was less interested. If Frank Procopio didn't want to talk to me, that was fine. Plenty of racing people liked talking racing. I'd talk to them instead.

The motivation to write this story didn't come from Dean, and it didn't come from the effort to find another angle and write another story. It came from an evening last month at Seekonk Speedway and a rare return to Seekonk of the Pro Four series. The night was planned as a tribute to Procopio, whose death last summer had come as a surprise to many in racing. The evening's pro-four race was billed as the first Frank Procopio Memorial. Unfortunately, it proved to be a bit of a yawner, as George Savary and Ed Holewiak made minced-meat out of a field that was thick with young drivers who hadn't been racing when the four-cylinder modifieds put on raucous shows at Seekonk and set lap times the Pro Stocks struggled to match.

What touched me instead about the evening was the reaction of many racers to the invitation to return to Seekonk and honor Procopio. The turnout of pro four cars was an impressive one, with most of the drivers who normally call Riverside Park home making the trip to Seekonk.

But more impressively, Dan Meservey and Joe Lemay returned to the series to race in Procopio's honor. Current pro stock driver Dick Houlihan paced the field with his NASCAR pro stock. And race winner Savary talked after the race about how important it was to win the race that was run in honor of Procopio.

And I didn't even know Frank Procopio. I confess, before I'd done some earlier work on the Pro Four series, and first gotten the assignment from Dean, I didn't even know *of* Frank Procopio. That's obvious by now to anyone who did. They know why Frank Procopio wouldn't talk to me. Thanks to a few of them, now I do, too.

Butch Ambrozio was one person who opened my eyes. Of all the friends that Frank Procopio left behind, Ambrozio, now the owner of the modified George's son Richard Savary races at Riverside Park, was among his closest.

When I related to Ambrozio my own experience in contacting Frank, he was less than surprised.

"That was just the way he was," said Ambrozio. "He was very to himself. He'd just rather see someone else get credit than get it himself.

"I guess he was the type of guy who figures he got his share. He always wanted to let some other guy get some.

"I knew him maybe 35 years. I've known him since I was a little boy. He was like a father to me."

Ambrozio relates some of Procopio's history as a car owner through the years, first campaigning midgets and later playing a paternal role in the evolution of four-cylinder stock car racing.

"He started in racing in the late forties or early fifties. That was before my time. But I heard plenty of stories. He stayed in the midgets until the mid-fifties, when all those shorttracks started closing down.

"Then in the sixties is when he got into the mini-stocks. Fellow name of Jimmy Dean was his driver. (The car was) a full-bodied Volkswagen with a two-barrel carburetor on the back of it. They ran maybe four or five years."

While Procopio raced his Volkswagen at the old Norwood Arena, a group of racers, many based on Cape Cod, were driving their VW-based racecars on the dirt at Lakeville. In 1972 word came that Norwood would be closing its gates. That bad news brought with it a change for mini-stock racing in New England, one that Procopio would work to make a positive one. One of those racers on Cape Cod remembers.

"Those were the years when we really had no direction," says Meservey, "except we wanted to go racing. I called Carl Merrill and Lou Modestino up at Oxford Plains. Carl told me that a bunch of ministock drivers were getting together: They were having a meeting . I think it was at Rose's Pizza in Brockton. There were a bunch of guys from the Norwood area. When that place closed, they had nowhere to go.

"As we talked, it seemed there were two people who were really focused. That was Frank and me. We both kind of felt that we had the same general goals and that we could go racing. That's how we got the whole thing started."

The "whole thing" was the club that came to be the New England Mini-Modified Association. As a force for the growth of the club, Procopio and Meservey were a potent team.

"I had the drive," says Meservey. "Frank had the direction. He was never much of a pusher, but if he wanted it to happen it happened."

What the two shared was, as Meservey said of the racers at Lakeville, they both wanted to go racing. That's not so special. But Frank Procopio was special because he wanted more than that, and not just for himself.

"He definitely wanted to win," says Ambrozio. "That's what he got excited about. But he'd help out the guy who wasn't winning. That's the kind of guy he was."

"He was very supportive of the mini-stocks," agrees Adrienne Venditti, who has taken over as Seekonk's promoter after the death of her father, Anthony. "He always sponsored cars. If someone didn't have the bucks to run for the night, he'd dig in and come up with it."

"If he had something to offer, he made sure you had it, if you needed a tire or whatever," says Houlihan, Procopio's driver for four successful seasons. "He did a lot of things nobody even heard he was doing."

Ambrozio remembers one example from his days as a car owner competing against Procopio at Westboro.

"He won the championship and won $500," says Ambrozio. "We came in second and won $300. He said, 'Why don't we just take empty envelopes and let them give the money to the guys in the back We won enough races this year. We won enough money.'"

The Venditti family saw a lot of Frank Procopio.

"He loved Seekonk," says Meservey. "That was his track. He had a lot of respect for Anthony and the Venditti family."

"My father didn't let too many people get close to him," says Adrienne. "But he would always stop and spend time with Frank no matter how busy he was. They had a lot of the same philosophies and they had a high level of respect for each other."

It was at Seekonk that the combination of Procopio and Houlihan became a force in mini-mod racing. You can imagine what it was like to drive for the man.

"He was probably like Joe Gibbs in a way," reflects Houlihan. "He knew how to get the right people and he knew how to motivate them. He just knew how to put a team together. Plus he was just the kind of guy you wanted to be around."

That theme is universal when someone is speaking of Frank Procopio.

"He was very quiet, humble – just a nice, nice man," says Adrienne Venditti.

"He was a hell of a nice guy," says Meservey. "A shirt-off-your-back kind of guy."

That seems to be the image that everyone is left with, more than his victories and championships, and there were a ton of both. More even than his numerous innovations, like his landmark Pinto-based mini as well as the Cavalier-bodied machine he introduced.

"He was one of those guys one step ahead," says Houlihan."For an older guy he had some pretty young ideas."

But innovators are a foregone conclusion in a sport as driven by technology as racing. The rarity is finding someone so strong that he can beat you and still go out of his way to help you beat him.

Life cheats you, I suppose, in a ton of ways. Losing the opportunity to get to know Frank Procopio is just one way for me. But in a world filled with way too many enemies and not even close to enough friends, nothing seems more unfair.

AUTHOR THOM RING covered racing for a number of daily newspapers across New England for over 20 years before publishing *Shorttrack* magazine, which featured the sport in the region. He's served as Technical Editor for *Trackside* magazine as well as a senior editor for *Late Model Racer* and New England Correspondent for *Late Model Digest*.

Ring was a race-winning kart driver and a solid back-of-the-packer in a dirt midget. He lives in Rhode Island with his wife, singer-songwriter Jan Luby.